S0-DFE-675

How to Put On a Horse Show

How to Put On

SOUTH BRUNSWICK AND NEW YORK:
A. S. BARNES AND COMPANY

a Horse Show

by
T. W. CARRITHERS

LONDON:
THOMAS YOSELOFF LTD

© 1971 by A. S. Barnes and Co., Inc.
Library of Congress Catalogue Card Number: 70-124197

A. S. Barnes and Co., Inc.
Cranbury, New Jersey 08512

Thomas Yoseloff Ltd
108 New Bond Street
London W1Y OQX, England

ISBN 0-498-07523-0
Printed in the United States of America

To Beth, my wife.
*Her subtle use of the spurs has
gotten me over many rough courses in life.*

Contents

Acknowledgments

I wish to thank those listed below for much help and inspiration. To many of them this book will come as a surprise, but unbeknownst to them, they had a hand in it. Thanks to George H. Cardinet, Jr., Tom P. Johnston, Kent Weaver, Bruce Lee, Dr. George Cardinet, III, DVM, Dr. Bill Throgmorton, DVM, Linda and Wentworth Tellington, Marie and Fred Kemm, Jack Costa, Betty and Jim Menefee, Marge Trimble, Chris Borba, O. L. "Red" Lott, Bob Vargas, Mrs. Ruth Becker, Dick Collins, Mr. and Mrs. Hermann Friedlaender, Col. Alex P. Sysin, Jack Huyler, Nancy McCall, Alan Ross, Graham Kislingbury, Ralph Walker, Mrs. Sandra McKeon, and Mr. James H. Blackwell, Executive Secretary of the American Horse Shows Association. And a further thanks to the late George Walling and the late Charles Broad, both of whom instructed me in the fine points of horse show management.

A special acknowledgment is given to the American Horse Shows Association for allowing me to quote from its publications. And many thanks to the organizations whose forms I have used as examples.

There are many others, both senior and junior, who have been a great help. To the many whose names have not been listed, but whose aid and assistance have not been forgotten—thanks.

Introduction

A horse show is an event at which owners, riders, and drivers can compete with one another in classes designed to allow a comparison among their horses—while performing in a manner inherent to all horses or to a specific breed—or a comparison among riders and drivers in their actions.

This definition just about covers all equine events: racing, rodeos, jumping, gymkhana, trail rides, equitation, harness affairs, halter and breeding shows, and other activities. And it covers all the combinations thereof.

Ever since the first horses were domesticated, men have gathered together to compare the merits of their animals. As civilization progressed, so did the number of uses to which the horse was put. This led to breeding for a specific purpose, which led to more comparisons. Hence the very beginnings of horse shows and events were in these matches of one horse against another.

From the early chariot drivers to the jousting knights, from military uses to the development of sporting events, men and horses have competed with other men and horses. At first these must have been casual affairs until the early Olympic Games, when horse events were actually scheduled and held. During the feudal era, jousting tournaments were a type of horse show where riders tried to unseat other riders from the great war horses that had been developed. The invention of gun powder and guns put an end to this kind of sport, but hunters of the

Western world took to the horse to pursue the fox, the wolf, and the stag.

In England hunting became very popular, and the breeding of horses turned toward a lighter and faster animal. Comparisons for speed led to racing in a formal fashion. In the meantime, in Europe, a certain type of riding and training developed that would school the horse and rider in highly complicated maneuvers to protect both in the contact of battle. From this came dressage.

On land the horse was man's main means of transportation. Carriage and draft horses were bred for size and strength. The great draft animals were slow compared to the lighter wagon horses, but each had its purpose. As breeds progressed, men looked for the best of each, for riding, driving, or both.

All of these early horse activities and uses channeled their way through time until, by the founding of our own country, the horse was in daily use in every community. We had racing before the Declaration of Independence; we had stage coaches; we had farm wagons; we had plow horses.

The first horse show of breeding classes, as we know them, in our country took place in June 1853 at Upperville, Virginia, when Col. Richard Hunter Dulaney exhibited his stallions and colts. This affair was continued yearly until the interruption of the Civil War. It was begun again in November 1869 and has been continuous since then.

In October 1883 the first modern horse show was held at Gilmore's Gardens, the forerunner to Madison Square in New York City. This show had over 250 horses, both pleasure and working types, the latter being the top draft horses of the time. Put on by the National Horse

Show Association of America, it grew to be quite a social event.

The American Horse Shows Association was founded in 1917, and formed a set of rules for shows and classes, along with standards of judging. Breed associations have been founded from time to time, each with its rules on standards and classifications. Most of these have been included in the American Horse Shows Association rule book. However, many of these groups sanction shows on their own, such as the American Quarter Horse Association, founded in 1940.

Since the turn of the century, there have been many developments in horse competitions. The Three Day, or Combined Event, was first held at the 1912 Olympic Games, being a comparison of the military use of the horse. Hunter Trials, the comparison of hunters over fences, came before this. Rodeos, where horse and rider compete in events developed from working cattle, became formalized around this time. Competitive trail riding came into being. Gymkhana events were evolved in various sections of the country. With the rise of the automobile age, the heavy draft horse suffered, but the light horse began to prosper, and the various types of horse and rider comparison—or horse events—also prospered.

In 1968 the American Horse Shows Association approved 825 shows, an increase of almost ten percent from the previous year. The American Quarter Horse Association sponsored over 1400 shows in 1968, a gain of over 100 from 1967. Other breed associations showed increases over the previous years. There can be no doubt that the pleasure horse population is on the increase, and with it the number of the various types of horse events.

The present-day horse shows are fun. They are fun for

the rider, fun for the owner, and fun for the spectator. And they can be fun for the people who put them on, if everyone knows his job and fully carries it out. Otherwise the event or show can become an unpleasant experience for everyone. A poorly planned and run affair disturbs the spectators, the exhibitors, and the management.

Successful events depend on capable managers, assisted by knowledgeable committees, diligent and unsparing in carrying out the smallest details. From the largest horse competitions down to the simplest one-day informal affairs, someone has the job of organizing and putting it on. This may vary from a single individual to a large committee, depending on the size and scope of the events. And that brings us to the point. Just how does anyone put on a horse show or horse event?

How to Put On a Horse Show

1

The Four Keys

Before a group, organization, club, or individual decides to put on a horse event, there are four key considerations involved: available experience, grounds, exhibitors, and finances. Each of these must be gone over carefully with much thought, for they will determine what kind of an event can be held and if it is feasible. All four keys are equally important, no matter what size of an affair one is considering. The larger the event the more complicated the planning, but just a small one-day playday takes the same four keys.

It is almost a necessity that someone in the group has had some experience with a horse show. In fact the more people who have had some connection with a horse event and can be included in the initial thinking, the better the final decision will be. Less will be left to chance. This experience may have come as an exhibitor, a manager, a secretary, an entry clerk, or in any capacity where he or she has been able to observe what went on. If no one has had any past connection with a show or horse affair, it is very advisable to go outside the group to find someone who is experienced and can furnish some guidance. The type of experience at hand will certainly influence the type of event to be considered.

Another vital key to the type of event is the location —available grounds. For a large show lasting several or more days an indoor arena may be desired. For a small one-day affair just an unfenced level area can be used. But the available grounds will have much weight when the final decision is made. Too often a show committee tries to put on an affair that is not suitable to the grounds.

It is necessary to check the size and location of the arena or arenas, stabling facilities, setup for concessions, sanitary arrangements, exhibitor and spectator parking, seating, water, trailer space, general convenience of the layout, and any other necessities for the type of show in mind. For instance, if it is a western show and cattle are to be worked, then fencing is quite important. If it is a combined training event, the terrain must lend itself to a cross-country course, and there must be a specified level area for a dressage ring. Each type of affair has special requirements that have to be considered.

Equipment is also considered when discussing available grounds. If jumps will be needed, then one should know where they will come from. If gymkhana is considered, then barrels, timing devices, poles, etc. have to be on hand. And there must be transportation to move equipment around and in and out of the arena.

Without sufficient exhibitors, there cannot be a successful horse event. Therefore, those who are thinking of putting on a show must also think about where the contestants will come from and what kind of classes they will show in. When a show is presented for the first time, there is no way of knowing how many exhibitors will enter; but by comparing the show to others that have been held in the same general area management will get some idea.

At the same time the exhibitors are being considered, it is well to check the dates, places, and types of other events in the surrounding vicinity. These data will have a definite effect on any decision about the affair. Conflicting dates have put more horse shows in the hole than poor management. However, always remember that certain types of events conflict very little with entirely different types of horse affairs. This is especially true for the smaller one-day events. For instance, a western show would draw very few exhibitors away from an English-type show in the same area and on the same date, but it would have quite an effect on a quarter horse affair under the same circumstances. Since a breed show will always draw from a larger area than a performance show, it is well to check for any specific show of the former kind within a greater geographical limit. From the exhibitor's viewpoint, there is no conflict among breed shows unless he raises more than one kind.

The fourth key is financing. At this point it is necessary to know how much money is available and where it will be coming from. No matter how large an event, or how small, there will be an initial outlay to get the show off the ground. And even a very small affair will have some expenses up to the time when entries start coming in. The bigger the event, the more the prior outlay will be.

There are several sources for the initial money needed. The show may be a financial benefit for a given charity. In this case, perhaps the beneficiary will help in the beginning, expecting to reap the income after expenses. If it is a club or other organization, it may have to dip into its treasury to cover such things as printing, ribbons and trophies, insurance, mailing, etc.

Again, the affair may be subsidized, such as a show

held in conjunction with a state fair or county fair. Here one has to know just how much commitment is available and exactly how it can be spent. These groups are usually governed by laws and rules set down by legislation, which are very specific concerning the use of money. Any show being so subsidized must stay within the framework of these regulations.

Shows that have been held from year to year (and have become fixtures) usually set aside enough of the income from each year to take care of the necessary preliminary expenses the following year. Any new management or new committee taking over from the old should check the finances on hand before any additions or changes are made in general format.

Just as different types of events appeal to spectators and exhibitors, so does the appeal of putting on a horse event vary with different groups. Hence, the sources of financing will also vary according to kinds of shows that are being considered. One certainly would not expect a club interested in Arabian horses to sponsor an Appaloosa breed show, nor would a junior club expect to attract the financial backing to put on a six-day affair.

No matter what kind of horse competition is under consideration, these four keys—experience, grounds, exhibitors, and finances—are of vital importance. An individual, group, or club is going to have to sell the idea to other individuals, or members of the group, in order to get the necessary support—especially if it is to be a charitable affair. The beneficiary must be convinced that the event will be successful and that there will indeed be benefits.

2

Type of Show

There are many types of horse competition, and each can have a number of divisions with a large selection of classes. An exhibitor can always find an affair at which he can show to his advantage. If he is a breeder, he will find halter classes for his particular kind of animal. If he is interested in competitive trail riding, he may find such a ride scheduled somewhere within his range. Hunter and jumper riders check events for their specialty. And so it goes.

Horse events can be roughly divided into flat or English saddle, western saddle, harness or driving, and halter or breeding affairs. And there can be a great number of combinations of these at one show. A large show, taking in several days or more, may have something for each type. A small, one-day event may cover only a segment of one type. Again, a show devoted to a single breed, such as Arabian, Welsh, or Morgan, may include classes in all four general classifications.

Flat saddle classes include equitation, pleasure, dressage, jumper, hunter and cross-country, saddle horses (three or five gaited), and trail riding. Western classes include equitation, pleasure, trail, stock horse (dry or

21

working cattle), cutting, roping, parade, and trail riding. Classes for harness or driving are those in which a two-wheeled bike or a four-wheeled vehicle is used. The latter may be wagons, buggies, road coaches, or viceroys. Halter classes are those in which the animal is shown in hand, such as model or breeding classes.

Almost all of the above can be divided further by age of rider, age of horse, sex of rider, sex of horse, height of animal, weight of animal, and by placing certain restrictions or qualifications on either the horse or rider or both. For example, events for amateur riders come under this category. Jumpers are now classified according to the amount of money won. Equitation classes are broken down by age of rider, such as 17 years and under, or 14 through 17 years of age. Competitive trail riding divides riders as to weight of contestant with equipment, and according to the experience of horse or rider. Gymkhana, in which the main division is for age of competitor, can be ridden with either type of saddle.

The simplest kind of an affair to hold is a one-day playday designed to attract local contestants. Another kind of easy show is a small schooling affair, where green horses are welcome and training tack is allowed. This sort of event will attract owners with animals not quite ready for the more formal shows. Even combined training events can be held with this in mind, by using lower level dressage tests and shortening the cross-country courses.

The largest type of affair to put on is one in which there is something for just about every show-minded exhibitor. It will include classes for almost every breed and in all manners in which they are shown. These are the big fixture shows that have developed over the years, such as the American Royal, the Grand National, the various state fairs, and others. Some even have shows within shows.

The American Horse Shows Association recognizes the following divisions in its current rule book: Appaloosa, Arabian, Combined Training, Dressage, Equitation, Hackney, Harness Pony, Hunter, Jumper, Junior Hunter and Jumper, Morgan, Palomino, Parade, Pinto, Pony of the Americas, Quarter Horse, Roadster, Saddle Horse, Shetland Pony, Tennessee Walking Horse, Welsh Pony, and Western. Each division has a number of class descriptions, and in some cases it is suggested that the particular breed (or other association) be written to for further classifications or types of competition.

From all this it can be seen that there is quite a choice in the type of horse events that can be held. This is why it is so important to consider the four keys: experience, grounds, exhibitors, and finances. Although the experience does not have to have been gained in the specific type of event in mind, it will certainly help. There is an amount of similarity among horse affairs and their management, even if the shows themselves are different.

Available places to hold shows or events will play a large part in the type of competitions. To hold a simple one-day western show, usually all that is needed is a good-sized arena with plenty of trailer parking space. But a competitive trail ride of even one day has to have 30 to 40 miles of trail, along with parking and stabling or tie-up facilities. Dressage needs a special size arena, while a combined training event not only needs a dressage arena, but available terrain from an outside course and a good ring with firm footing for jumping.

No matter what kind of an affair is decided upon, unless it will draw exhibitors it will be a failure. As mentioned before, a check of the other affairs held in the same area will show what kind of competitions appeal to the most and bring the largest entries. Horsemen are gregarious and tend to go where other horsemen go, and they also have the inclination to enter as many classes as they can. These are things to think about when deciding what kind of a show to hold.

Finances have been gone over before, but a word of caution is due. Always be prepared in case the event loses money. Someone—an individual, a group, or a club—must underwrite the show. Many unforeseen misfortunes can happen. Poor weather may affect the attendance of exhibitors and spectators. An epidemic may hit the horse population of the area and cut the entries. Disasters are not common, but they can happen and they can be very unfavorable to the financial outcome of the event.

Having gone over the four considerations, and the types of events that might be held, the group, club, or individual decides to put on a certain kind of competition.

3

The Committee

Having decided to hold a horse event and having determined the kind to have, the group or club's next step is to appoint a committee. There are several ways to do this. One is to appoint or elect a chairman and let him select the necessary members to complete the committee. Another is to appoint the chairman and also the committee.

Organizations and clubs that hold several events during the year will do well to choose a separate chairman for each affair. For instance, one chairman could take charge of horse shows, while another could handle combined training events. A chairman with more than one show during the year could choose a separate committee for each, thereby spreading the work load.

There are organizations that are formed to put on a certain horse event annually. In their formation, they hopefully have included several members who are well experienced in that particular field. Such organizations are usually set up so that they are the committee, and each member is expected to contribute his particular talents to one of the required phases. Where there is a particular cause or beneficiary for the event, the committee will probably include at least one representative for that element.

The governing body of any group putting on a horse event is responsible for the proper operation of the affair. It may delegate its authority to a committee or a chairman, but it is still responsible for the final outcome. Therefore some care should be exercised in the selection of the chairman and his committee, since they actually conduct the event.

In small shows of the one- or two-day variety, the chairman is usually also the manager. It is his responsibility to draw up the classifications and the prize list, get the necessary judges, stewards, and licenses, arrange for the mailing of the entry forms, see that the grounds are available, and check many other items prior to the show. In Appendix P there is a check list that will help a manager in his duties and those he may wish to delegate to members of the committee.

A professional manager should be hired for big events taking five or more days to complete. There are a number of these gentlemen available and they have one thing going for them—experience. Any group putting on a large event can always find a professional manager who has handled a similar affair in the past. And for a fee, he will be glad to manage the group's coming venture. Fees vary depending on the size and scope of the show, and they are set forth in the contract between the sponsoring group and the manager usually after negotiation.

When there is an overall chairman for a big affair, the manager has less responsibility, since many of his duties prior to the event are handled by committee members, directly under the chairman. For instance, the duty of renting and preparation of the grounds would be given to a subcommittee for a large show; however, for a smaller one the manager would handle this directly.

It boils down to the fact that the larger the event, the more people it takes to put it on. The chairman is the coordinator, who must tie together all the various parts and make sure all the necessary jobs are being carried out. The smaller the event, the less people it takes. Hence, the chairman can also operate as the manager since the picture is not so big that he cannot see all of it.

After selecting the method of management and choosing a manager, the next and equally important position to fill is that of secretary. In small one- or two-day affairs, the secretary can also act as the entry clerk. However, in larger shows where the entries will number from 600 up, it is best to have a separate entry clerk. Too, in a large affair there will be much correspondence with sponsors and associations, contracts to prepare, program to put together, and many other items for which a secretary is needed. So the additional work of an entry clerk should not be included in her duties.

This is not to say that the secretary has nothing to do with the entry clerk; they both work together. The secretary will be responsible for the preparation of the entry book, work sheets, judges' cards, exhibitors' numbers, etc. And if it is a large recognized show she will have to acknowledge the receipt of all entries. But having a separate person handling the receiving and entering of the exhibitors will be an immense help to a secretary.

If a show or horse event is sanctioned by a particular association, or by more than one, the secretary will find in its current rule books a list of things that he or she is required to do. Among these is sending the show results to the sanctioning group as soon as possible after the show is over. The allowed time will vary among associations so it is necessary to check for each one. This mailing of results is very important and the failure to do so may very well endanger future sanctions.

Each association, whether it is local, state-wide, or national, has awards for highest scoring riders and horses in certain categories. The exhibitors are very interested in getting credit for any points that they may have acquired at that show. Hence it is only fair to them to abide by the rules of that group. This applies to breed shows as well as open affairs.

A good horse event secretary is worth her weight in uranium. She has her own check list and makes sure everything is ready on time. She should be able to type and handle people graciously. A secretary who can help a misguided exhibitor out of a quandary with a smile will have made a friend, and an exhibitor who will return to future events. If possible, a committee chairman or manager should choose a secretary with experience in the kind of event being put on. If this is not possible, try to select one that will be available in the future, where the experience gained in this affair will be useful.

The next key position is that of treasurer. In a large affair any amount from $5,000 up may come in and out of the show account. Someone must be in control of this money, and this should be the treasurer. In a club that puts on affairs, the club's treasurer may act in kind for the show. Groups that are formed to handle one or two large shows a year will have a treasurer for these. In a small one- or two-day affair, the secretary or manager may act as the treasurer also. But no matter how large or how small a show or event is, all incoming and outgoing money must be accounted for. When all accounts are settled, the treasurer prepares a financial report for the club, group, or whoever is sponsoring the show. If it is for the benefit of some cause, the beneficiary also gets a statement.

Some organizations set up a show account. Others may lump it in with their general account. Some management groups keep a separate show account for each year. If the affair is being subsidized, such as a fair or the like, the treasurer will very likely be appointed by the governing body behind the subsidy.

One of the main duties of the treasurer is to see that the budget for the event is followed. Even the smallest horse affair has to have a budget of some kind, even if it is written on the back of an old envelope. Large events have a voluminous budget with many entries. The treasurer lets each subcommittee head know exactly what money has been allotted to his section of the operation, and any deviation over and above this figure should be cleared with the treasurer. Since he is in the position to see the whole financial picture, he will know best where savings are being made to balance overages in other sections.

As a rule, the manager, the secretary, and the treasurer are the first committee people chosen. There will be many subcommittees, with the chairman of each as a member of the show committee. For smaller events, many of the subcommittees may be combined. Roughly, these include ribbons and trophies, grounds, ring management, program, publicity, hospitality, admissions, concessions, stable management, and first aid. These will be explained later.

There is one thing every event must have: an address and a telephone number. A small event may use the address and phone number of the secretary or manager, while a large show may actually rent office space and set up headquarters. All advertising, flyers, premium lists, and entry blanks should carry this address and phone number. Interested exhibitors and spectators will want to know where they can get further information about the coming event.

4

Show Date and Sanctions

Selecting the dates for the event is most important so as not to conflict with other horse activities that might draw from the same field of exhibitors. Although the number of horses and contestants is growing each year, so is the number of horse shows and other activities. Too many similar affairs scheduled at the same time in the same area hurt the attendance of each. Thus the choice of dates must be checked against the dates of other known shows or events within the drawing range of the selected type of affair.

Big shows of five to ten days have fixed dates that have been established by custom over the years. Any new venture of a like nature will have to find a time that will be most convenient for everyone concerned. Smaller affairs are held on weekends, where the competition for dates is quite keen. New clubs and organizations are formed as the number of horsemen increases, and each wants to hold some kind of an event. Hardly a weekend goes by during the open weather season when there are not two or more horse events in an area.

There are several ways to check ahead of time if certain dates will be open. Look to see when the previous year's shows were held. This involves getting hold of last year's horse magazines—breed and general—and looking through their show calendar sections. The American Horse Shows annual rule book publishes the dates of all its sanctioned shows for the past year and its monthly publication, *Horse Show,* reports changes in the current year. The *Quarter Horse Journal* has an excellent calendar, as does the *Chronicle of the Horse.* All organizations that sanction shows or events put out bulletins about their activities that list coming events to be held under their sponsorship.

Even a small one-day affair can run into trouble if it is held at the same time another local event is scheduled. It may be necessary to get on the telephone and check around with other groups to make sure there is no conflict. Because of various conflicts, clubs and organizations have formed associations in areas that act as a clearing house for show dates. This was one of the main reasons for the formation of the American Horse Shows Association back in 1917.

There are many associations throughout the country that sanction horse events, the American Horse Shows Association being the best known as far as horse shows go. There are associations for trail rides, combined training, dressage, breeds, hunters and jumpers, cutting horses, and many others. In almost every one of these, points are awarded to horses and riders who win at events sanctioned by that particular association. Many shows are licensed by more than one of these groups, holding classes acceptable to each. Hence they will appeal to a larger number of exhibitors.

Each of these associations has its own rules about the distance between shows held on the same date, what classes must be held, what judges must be used, and many other points. If a show committee is considering obtaining a sanction from a particular group, it should get the most recent rule book of that group to see what its requirements are. It may be that the selected dates will be in conflict, in which case the sanctioning association will not grant its approval.

It is always a drawing card for a show to have the sanction of at least one of the associations. This will bring exhibitors who are members of the authorizing group and who are competing for points. It also tells the contestants that the show will be run according to the rules of that association, and also that the judge or judges are qualified according to those rules.

Very large events will have the sanction of a number of groups so as to appeal to a large number of contestants. They will have hunters, jumpers, breeds, and any other special licensing faction. Each exhibitor can find an association that covers his specific forte and he will usually go where it is recognized. Hence the large affairs try to cater to as many as possible.

Some events, especially breed shows, will stay only with the breed association. This is true of the Quarter Horse, the Appaloosa, the Shetland, the Arabian, etc. If there are enough exhibitors of a single breed in an area, then the event will have a good chance of success. The rules of these groups include many classes so than an affair may be held completely within the rules, in both halter and performance divisions.

Some smaller shows may decide to go ahead without any specific license. In such cases they will get many exhibitors who do not feel up to the bigger affairs. They will do well to schedule classes appealing to that type of contestant, but they must still try to avoid conflicting dates. Another small affair in the same area at the same time may play havoc with the entries.

As mentioned before, there are many associations that sanction horse events and activities. In the Appendix is a list of the larger and better known groups. Some of these are national in scope; others cover a specific locality. Some are breed groups; some apply to certain types of performing animals; and some have local chapters. It is best to write directly to parent organizations for information concerning rules, licenses, sanctions, and the like.

5

Judges and Stewards

Once the show or event dates are set and the desired sanctions are obtained, the committee must engage the necessary judges and stewards. Usually the manager makes the actual contact and gets the commitment from these officials.

Most of the associations that license horse activities have a list of judges and stewards who are qualified under the rules of that organization. The American Horse Shows Association list is by far the most extensive, with over 1500 names in its 1969 rule book. Some of these are certified in many divisions and some are specialists concentrating in a particular division or breed. Many of the breed organizations have a separate list of judges qualified for use in events and shows sanctioned by them, and will furnish this roster upon request.

If the show or horse activity is being licensed by one or several of the associations, be sure the judges and stewards that the committee may want are acceptable to those groups. There are times when the manager or committee knows that a judge is capable of handling the event but does not have a license from a particular association. In this case, the association may grant a special judge's card for that event or show if the management so asks. In some groups there is a fee for such a card, and the show committee assumes responsibility for the qualifications of that judge. The same applies to stewards.

Some of the sanctioning groups do not require a licensed judge, but allow the committee to choose anyone it wishes. These organizations go on the premise that any judge who satisfies the committee is acceptable to them. Once in a while an inexperienced person is asked to judge, but if he or she is capable and consistent, the exhibitors will accept the decisions without complaint. However, a poor judge will leave a bad taste with the contestants and the reputation of the affair will suffer.

To get a license to judge in any division or breed, a person must go through quite a period of qualifying. In almost all cases, the prospective judge has been a breeder, exhibitor, or trainer, or has had extensive exposure to the divisions in which he wishes to be considered. The American Horse Shows Association asks that the applicant fill out a questionnaire, giving qualifications, background, and previous experience, along with the names of recognized judges or members of the Association who are familiar with his work. The Association then sends out questionnaires to those named by the applicant, and it must get back at least six replies, of which three must be from judges already licensed in the divisions applied for. Most breed associations have a similar procedure. Therefore, if a judge's name appears in the American Horse Shows Association list or in a similar list put out by any specific horse organization, it can be assumed that he is capable of judging the divisions or breeds stated after his name.

In order to remain on the list a person has to judge at

least one show within a given time. The reputation of inefficient judges soon spreads and they will not be invited to perform often enough to stay on the active list.

Big shows with many classes and different arenas going on at the same time will use several judges. Small one- or two-day affairs may use just one qualified judge who may be recorded or registered in all the types of events the show will have. (They may also use a capable beginning judge who has not yet applied for recognition.)

Each show committee should get its judges well ahead of time. There are many very proficient judges who are quite popular with exhibitors in their divisions and breeds. There is a heavy demand on their services and they are booked far in advance. To get one of these people, contact should be made as soon as possible or he may be already engaged. A phone call may be more expensive than a letter, but time is important. An invitation and an acceptance by phone can always be verified by letter within a few days.

Stewards are very important to a show or other horse activity. Their job is to represent the sanctioning association, see that its rules are obeyed, and represent the management, the judges, and the exhibitors. They have no power to make a ruling, but are asked to make recommendations to the show committee in event of a complaint. They act as a buffer between the exhibitors and the management or the judge. A good steward anticipates any trouble and heads it off. He must have a thorough knowledge of the rules of the association he represents and possess a great deal of tact.

Most sanctioning organizations require the show or event to have a steward. Some, like the American Horse Shows Association, furnish a roster of stewards from which to choose. As with judges, a committee may select a person not on the list to act as steward and will have to get a special steward's card for that particular affair. Other associations will require a steward but will allow the show committee to pick a knowledgeable person, relying on the committee's good judgment. And a few other associations do not request a steward. In this case it is still wise to ask someone to act as show steward. When it comes to the interpretation of the rules, a good steward can forestall a difference of opinion between management and exhibitors.

When a show or a horse event is over, most associations that require a steward ask that he furnish them with a written conduct report of the affair. Many use a set form, similar to the one used by the American Horse Shows Association. It is quite comprehensive and covers all facets of the affair from the physical layout to personnel. There is a time limit for sending in the report, usually three days from the end of the affair.

There are two rather important items in the steward's report. One is his rating of the show, and the other is any suggestions he may have given the management to improve the event. An unsatisfactory rating may mean a conditional approval for a future event. To avoid such a mark, the committee and everyone connected with the management should be very careful to follow all the rules and to cover completely all phases of the activity.

Capable stewards are in demand and many do a number of shows per year. They have experience in many types of horse events and are exposed to all kinds of management. They are in a position to give advice and help the committee with suggestions not only for the present affair but for the future. The best ones seldom give unasked-for guidance, but they are willing to make helpful recommendations when asked.

There is no set remuneration for judges and stewards. It is a matter of negotiation. Inquiries into other clubs or groups as to what they have paid their judges and stewards may be of some help. With many officials the fee will depend on the type of show, the number of classes to be judged, and the physical demands made on them. A large show, taking five days or a week or more, with licenses from several associations, may pay a judge a daily fee or a flat fee for the whole show. Also there is the matter of expenses and travel allowances. The fees and expenses should be discussed at the very first contact with a judge or a steward. It may determine whether the show can afford him or not.

Smaller shows may obtain an unlicensed judge or a beginning one. He will expect a fee, although not as large as a recognized judge for a sanctioned show. It is still a matter of negotiation. But remember, he is giving his time and experience, and unless he offers his services for free he should be made a decent offer.

There are times when the affair is for a benefit or a cause, and every penny raised will go to a very special purpose. If others who would normally get paid are volunteering their services, this fact could be relayed to a prospective judge or steward, asking him if he will donate his abilities for expenses only. This is done on occasion, but only for a most worthy cause.

Great care should go into the selection of the judges and stewards for any event. The committee should get together and choose several possibilities in case one or more are not available. Certain judges are quite popular and will draw more exhibitors than others. Some do not like to operate too close to home; others make no exceptions. Remember, a trainer cannot judge any of his pupils, so a trainer who is a judge will do better outside of his own area. These are some of the points to consider when selecting a judge.

6

Prize List and Entry Blank

Prize lists—or premium lists—and entry forms come in various sizes, depending on the event. A very large affair, taking a week or more with several hundred classes, will usually put out a premium list in booklet form, running over 100 pages. A small one-day affair such as a schooling show can get by with a single sheet.

For many types of affairs a separate entry blank will be used, requiring information that will be included in a catalog to be published for the show. A single-page prize list will have an entry form at the bottom of the page.

The rule books of any approving associations will state what each requires to be published in the premium list. It will vary from association to association, but there will be certain facts that must be covered.

In the Appendix there are examples of pages from a large affair, a single-page prize list, and a check list that can be used for almost any type of horse affair. However, an explanation is needed for each heading.

1. *Name of the Affair*

This is the name and type of show or competition. Well-known events such as the American Royal, the Grand National, and others need only the name to tell the type of affair. But a small show will want to say whether it is a western, gymkhana, trail ride, junior, open, combination, or what type. An example is Seven Oaks Stables 5th Annual Quarter Horse Show, or the Rough Riders Annual Playday. A prospective exhibitor will be attracted to his type of event and will be more likely to look through the prize list if the type appeals to him.

2. *Date and Place*

The place is the actual location of the affair. If it is a well-established arena, the name may be sufficient, but it is best to give the address and, if necessary, directions on how to find it. Some premium lists will carry a sketch or a small map of the area.

3. *Judges and Stewards*

The name of the judge (or judges), the divisions that each will judge, and where each is from should be in the first part of the list. Exhibitors are most interested in who will be officiating. The name (or names) of the stewards, if there is more than one, must be given. As mentioned before, the contestants will want to know to whom to turn when they have questions on the show operations. A small one-day, one-type of competition can get by with the statement that the name of the judge will be announced later, but it is to the show's advantage to definitely name the judge.

4. *Approvals and Sanctions*

A list of all approvals and sanctions must be given so that the contestants will know what competitions are open to them. If they are competing for points in a certain association, they will want to know if the show has the approval of that group. Some sanctioning associations such as the American Horse Shows Associations require that a special form be included in the premium list, as do certain others, and their rule books will provide the necessary information.

5. *Rating of Affair*

To obtain a specified rating under the rules of various groups, a competition must fulfill a given set of requirements. Perhaps part of the competition has one rating and part another. This must be stated and usually is included in the section under sanctions and approvals.

6. *List of Officials*

In a large affair, this can be a complete list of every committee member, a list of the officers of the sponsoring group, and everyone connected with the show and his function. In a small event it may be just the secretary. But if it is to be a comprehensive list, make certain everyone is included.

7. *Schedule of Events*

There must be a timetable for the affair, showing the starting hour for each session—morning, afternoon, and evening—and the sequence of classes given. Exhibitors realize that this is all tentative and any changes will be furnished to them in plenty of time. In large shows where there are many classes in each division, such as jumper, hunter, and breed, the premium list will give a separate schedule of classes by section or division, in addition to a straight timetable.

A lot of thought has to be put into the schedule. Even at a one-day affair, a contestant who is eligible for the first or second class does not want to wait if his next class is one of the last on the program. This is just as true for shows taking several or more days to run. Also the spectators must be considered. Events having the

most appeal should be put on at times when the most ob-
servers can be present. And these should be planned with
the least inconvenience to the competitors.

8. *Class or Event Specifications*

Most associations that give show approvals require that
the specifications of each class or event be spelled out.
This is for several reasons. The judge will know exactly
what he is to look for, the exhibitor will know what he
is expected to do, and the spectator will know what to
watch for. The rule book of each sanctioning group will
give the exact description of each class and how it should
be written.

Many small one-day affairs will merely name a class
without giving a full description. Somewhere in the prize
list there will be a statement as to the rules under which
the show is held. This leaves it up to the contestant to
be sure he knows the specifications for that particular
event. If there is to be any variance, the prize list should
say so.

9. *Entry Fees*

Each class or event must have a statement regarding
the charge for entering. This can be done in several ways.
It may be put in along with the specifications for each
class, or it may be a blanket statement for all classes.
Again, it may be the same for all classes except certain
ones that can be listed separately. In events where there
are money prizes, the entry fee statement should explain
if part of it will be added back and be made a portion
of the award.

Somewhere in the premium list there should be the
policy of the management concerning the return of entry
fees in case the exhibitor is unable to attend. Such a
statement will solve a lot of problems that always arise.

Some affairs have a no-refund policy under any circumstances. Others are more lenient, requiring a veterinarian's or doctor's certificate.

10. *Post Entry Policy*

Whether or not to take post entries is a decision of the management that must be given in the prize list. Large shows or affairs that publish a catalogue or program for sale to the public or to the exhibitors will not take post entries. Since they will list all the horses and contestants in the catalogue, they must know them definitely by the time it goes to press. There is nothing more disconcerting to a spectator than to see a number on a contestant and not find it in his program, especially if it happens to be a ribbon winner.

Small one- and even two-day affairs will usually take post entries. This enables competitors who have been doubtful to come at the last minute and helps the affair financially, since there is always a small additional charge above the entry fee.

11. *Closing Date*

This should be prominently stated in the premium list, preferably in more than one place, and must also be printed in the entry form. Shows that publish a catalogue for sale or distribution to the public will set a closing date far enough ahead so that all entries can be included in the publication. Smaller affairs will usually set a closing date just enough time ahead so as to give the secretary the opportunity to complete her work sheets. Even shows that take post entries will set a closing date and any entries received after that time will be considered as post entered.

12. *Description of Courses*

Many large shows will include a drawing of the jumper

and hunter courses for the benefit of the exhibitors. Although this is not an absolute requisite, it is certainly a help to prospective contestants, especially the juniors. Some of these drawings are rather elaborate, while others may be quite simple.

13. *Map or Sketch of Show Location*

If any event is being held at a place that is unfamiliar to many exhibitors, a sketch or map showing how to get to the grounds may be included. This is especially true if the location is new.

14. *Specific Rules Applying to the Show or Event*

No two affairs are exactly alike. Hence any specific rules that will hold for this affair should be stated in the prize list. These may include the number of entries necessary to fill a class, the show's policy in event of class cancellation, the combining of classes, etc. Any ground rules that will apply must be given.

15. *General Information*

The catchall section of the premium list is where the information on stabling, trailer parking, availability of feed and bedding, food concessions, exhibitor housing, entertainment, etc. is stated. Anything that has not previously been covered will be set forth in this section.

The entry form or blank will be a separate sheet for most affairs. However small shows that put out a single sheet prize list may place it on the same page. No matter which, there are certain data the entry secretary will need: the name of the horse, the rider, the owner, and the class entered, along with the entry fee. There is almost always a release clause that does not hold the show committee, the owners of the grounds, and any other show officials responsible for loss or damage to the entrant. The entry blank will have the closing date stated on it, the secretary's name, address, and phone number, and to whom checks are made payable. There must be a space for the exhibitor's signature, or the guardian in case of a junior.

In the Appendix are several examples of entry forms, both those printed separately and those included on the same sheet as the premium list.

Some consideration should be given to the size and form of the entry blank for affairs that expect a large number of entrants. It is a help to the entry secretary to be able to file these in a loose-leaf notebook, apart from all her other papers. Some entry secretaries will use a file of manila folders, arranged so that the entries may be placed in alphabetical order.

After all the necessary information to be contained in the prize list and entry blank is delivered to the printer, and he is told which form to use, he will set up the data for a print run. But before he does any printing, some-one—usually the show manager—will proofread the premium list and entry form. This is an absolute must, since any error found after the distribution of the forms must be corrected. This often involves a lot of work, inconvenience, and additional costs. So the time to catch any errors is before the lists and blanks are printed.

The actual number of prize lists and entry blanks to be printed will be determined by the expected distribution. This in turn is figured out from the size of the mailing lists plus any additional copies that will be sent to stables, saddle shops, and other places where interested horsemen might pick up one.

There are several ways to get a good mailing list. One is to borrow one from a successful affair of the same type. Another source is the mailing list of a sanctioning association. Some require that the show mail its prize list and entry form to its membership. Shows that have been held over a period of years will build up a mailing list based on their entries from previous affairs. Another method is to get the programs of other shows, which will have an index of exhibitors, and build a mailing list from these.

Small one-day affairs may not mail out their prize lists but will distribute them to trainers, stables, other clubs, and tack shops. They will rely on local publicity and word of mouth to advertise the show.

Events that advertise in horse publications will get a certain number of inquiries, some of which will actually attend the affair. A prospective exhibitor who is a new-comer to an area will inquire around so as to get his name on the various mailing lists. He may even join an association or a club just to get prize lists.

Once a mailing list is started, it needs constant attention. Old riders drop out; new ones come up; addresses are changed. A list that has not been used for a year may have changed as much as 20 percent.

The cost of mailing must be considered. First class mail is the most expensive, but will guarantee forwarding in case of a change of address, or return in case of not being able to be delivered. For very large lists, a bulk mailing permit may be used. This may be obtained from the local post office and is cheaper for large mailings. It has several disadvantages, one of which is that all mail must be packaged together by zip code numbers. This means that the mailing list must be arranged accordingly.

Third class mail is the least expensive way to mail individual prize lists and entry blanks. But unless the mailing list is up to date, somewhere between 10 and 20 percent will not reach the addressee, since this kind of mail will not be forwarded.

A good mailing list of active exhibitors is a valuable article for any show management to have. It is well worth the trouble to begin and to cultivate, especially for the type of event that a committee feels itself best suited to put on.

7

Important Jobs

The following are key positions in which the best available help you can get is needed. Each has an important role to play in the success or failure of the show. The show manager should give careful consideration to each job and pick the most qualified people.

Show Veterinarian

Every show must have a veterinarian. The small one-day affairs should make arrangements to have one on call. Larger shows, or sanctioned shows, are required to have one present during the show. His duties are outlined in the various association rule books, and he should be available to assist the judge in the determination of an unsound horse. He is also there in case of an accident or any other equine emergency.

Although you may ask him to donate his time, it is usual to offer him remuneration, since his time is valuable to him and he is giving up his calls for the time of the show.

Blacksmith

Some sponsoring associations require a blacksmith to be present during the show. At any rate he will be there at the request of the management. He is paid for any shoeing he does by the owner of the horse in question.

Announcer

His job is to call in the classes, give the change of movements, and announce the results. He explains what is going on for the benefit of the spectators. He should have direct communication with the in gate man and with the entry clerk so he knows if a horse is scratched. He is a valuable adjunct to the show and should be knowledgeable concerning the type of show and its classes.

In gate Man

He has one of the key jobs in the show. He lines up the incoming classes and has them ready to go when called. He has the order of going in individual performance classes (such as jumpers) and sends them in without delay. By being fast and efficient he keeps the show moving along.

Ringmaster

He is an aide to the judge, and transmits the judge's requests to the announcer for the class. He sees that the class runs smoothly, doesn't converse with the judge unnecessarily, and makes sure the judge has a judging card for the class. He works with the jump crew in setting up the courses and checking their heights.

Jump Crew or Ring Crew

Large shows usually have a hired crew to set up jumps, rake the ring, replace fallen jumps, etc., but small shows rely on volunteer help, which is usually hard to come by. It is a thankless task, and yet has to be done. Good planning can cut down on a ring crew's work and make it easier for them. This is a help when you are asking for volunteers.

Course Designer and Supervisor

Shows that include jumper, hunter, cross-country, or trail classes should have one individual in charge of them.

He must know what equipment he has available, the limits of the terrain, and the type of competition he can expect. He will try to make his course designs fit the degree of ability of the exhibitors and their horses. The rule books of various associations may have suggestions on course designing and even drawings and illustrations to help. But here again, there is no substitute for experience.

The above described positions are vital in the actual running of the affair. Smoothness of operation depends on each and his relation and cooperation with the others of the group. For a big affair, running four or five days or more, it would not be remiss to have a meeting of these key people on the grounds to go over the duties of each for the benefit of all. A dry run or a rehearsal will help immensely.

8

Subcommittees

As mentioned before, there may be a number of sub-committees. Each of these will have a specific job to do in connection with a necessary phase of the operation. For smaller events some of these may not be too important, but for large shows or affairs, each subcommittee will need to be big enough to do a good job.

Ribbons and Trophies

Once the prize list is drawn up, it is an easy matter to see just what ribbons and trophies are needed. Each class will have a prize of some kind to be awarded. In some events it may be money, which will include ribbons but not necessarily a trophy. One of the duties of this committee is to be sure that perpetual or challenge trophies are on hand, having been returned by previous winners, and to have replicas made where necessary.

There are many manufacturers of ribbons and trophies, advertising in various horse publications. They all have catalogs available and it is a good idea to have a few of these on hand to get an idea of the costs involved when the show budget is being set up. For a group putting on its first affair, it is wise to shop around. Other shows of longer standing usually have settled on one source, and these facts will be passed on to new members of the committee.

There is one very important job that can be delegated to this subcommittee, or it may be considered so important to the particular show that it is made a separate and distinct task. This is the business of obtaining sponsorships. In established affairs, certain events may have had the same sponsors over the years. But these will still have to be gotten in touch with to verify their continued support. New events may have been added to the show and sponsors should be solicited for these.

Although the job of obtaining sponsors has been included here under ribbons and trophies, many large affairs, especially benefit shows, will do well to set up a separate subcommittee for this purpose. Where an affair is being held for a specific benefit or organization, the task of obtaining sponsorships is usually delegated to a member of the benefitting group. He is in a better position to ask for such donations in the name of the beneficiary.

Grounds

The subcommittee on grounds has charge of the physical setup of the affair, except for the actual arenas and rings. It takes care of communications, necessary lighting, all parking, seating, sanitary facilities, and the setting up of the show office. Included in the parking is that for exhibitors, trailers, officials, spectators, and the location of first aid setup. The grounds committee sees to the public address system and all other communication between announcers, secretaries, back gate, etc. It also plans the location of booths and concessions and sees that they have the needed utilities present.

Ring Management

This group is made up of the gate men, the ring crew,

the announcer, the ringmaster, the course designer, and any other person involved with the actual operation of the conduct of the show within the rings. This group has charge of all the special equipment that is needed for any class, such as timing devices, jump material, gymkhana gear, watering equipment, and means for dragging the arenas. The preparation of the arenas for each class is the responsibility of this committee. The speed and efficiency with which this group works is extremely important to the success of the whole show.

Program or Catalogue

The job of this subcommittee is the makeup, printing, and distribution of the program. This includes the solicitation of advertising, which is very vital in determining the actual cost of the program or catalogue.

Every large show will have a program that is sold to the public as well as the exhibitors. The number printed and distributed will determine the fees charged to advertisers. Most large affairs will engage a professional to take charge of the program from beginning to end. Some show managements will undertake this project themselves. Many small one- or two-day shows will not use a program, but merely use their prize list with a supplement sheet containing a list of the exhibitors. However, certain sanctioning associations will require that the show have a catalog or program if its rating is in a given bracket. A good catalogue will include everything that is in the prize list, along with a list of the horses, their descriptions, owners, and riders. All of this is of interest to the spectators and the contestants, and will help sell the programs.

Where a professional is used, there are several ways of handling the finances. He may do the job for a set fee with all sales of the catalogues going to the benefit of the show. He may do it for a percentage of the advertising fees, again with all sales money going to the show. Or he may merely guarantee that the show will have a catalogue in sufficient numbers to meet the demand, and take all the proceeds himself. If a professional is engaged, a contract that will spell out in detail the responsibilities of both parties must be drawn so as to avoid any future misunderstandings.

If a show management decides to handle the program itself, it is well to use the same printer or printing source that did the prize list. Since the catalogue contains almost the same information that is in the premium list, it is easier and cheaper for the same printer to do both.

Publicity

This is another phase of the operation of a show that may be handled by a hired professional or by the show management itself. Publicity has a threefold objective. It is directed at the public to draw spectators, at the exhibitors to induce them to attend, and at advertisers to assure them of the affair's exposure. For a large show with plenty of spectator space, a professional may be needed to cover all the publicity outlets in trying to attract the public's attendance. A small show may rely on short notices in the local press.

Here again, a professional public relations firm or individual will require a contract that will tell what he will try to do and how he will go about it. The management always has the problem of balancing the cost of the publicity with the actual return in the way of spectator and exhibitor attendance. For any new venture, this is always nebulous until after the show. For an established fixture, experience has shown what can be anticipated, and the budget is set accordingly.

Advertising in horse magazines and publications is directed at prospective contestants, while newspaper, radio, and television announcements are directed at increasing the public attendance. Posters, if put out early enough, are directed at both.

There are many important points to stress when publicizing an affair. There may be a famous horse or rider; the judge may have some special attribute; the beneficiary of the show may be noteworthy. There are several ways of publicizing the show, and a professional will dig these out. But the management, or committee, will have to figure out its own hooks to hang pictures and prose on.

Another thing to consider is a press party, either for lunch or cocktails, to which the press is invited and given exposure to all favorable aspects of the event. A meeting between the press and the management is very helpful in getting the right coverage for the show.

One other consideration is a press booth or location at the show itself. Those covering the event will always appreciate a place where they can sit down, write their stories, or phone them in. Good relationships gained this way pay dividends in full.

Hospitality

The job of this subcommittee is to make the exhibitors feel that they are wanted at the show. It makes arrangements for hotel and motel accommodations, sets up and handles any special parties for the judges and exhibitors, and provides transportation. Anything that is on the social side of the affair is managed through this committee. In small affairs the manager and the secretary do this job.

In very large events with a heavy social schedule a fair-sized committee will be required to take care of the details.

Admissions

Many large affairs, especially those held for the benefit of some cause or philanthropy, rely on advance ticket sales in raising funds for the show's success. This is in addition to ticket sales at the time of the show. Seating accommodations at the show determine if general, reserved, and box seats can be sold. A committee must be set up to handle these sales.

Some smaller events do not have any special seating arrangements and therefore have no admission charge. Others that can control the parking may extract a fee for each auto admitted to the grounds. There are several ways of charging admission that should be considered when setting up the show's budget.

Concessions

There are two types of concessions with which a show may concern itself. One is mandatory: the food and refreshment setup. The other type is the miscellaneous kind such as tack booths, manufacturers' booths, and the like.

No matter how long a show is expected to run, food and refreshments must be available to contestants and spectators. Such accommodations should be open at least an hour before the beginning of the show each day and should remain open until after the close in the evening.

There are several ways of handling the food concession. It may be most convenient to engage an outside caterer who will take care of the whole food setup, paying the show a percentage of his gross. Some clubs or groups that are putting on a show may want to take care of the food situation themselves. There are always local clubs that will take care of the food concession in order to raise money for their own purposes. This is true where there are many horse clubs or groups in an area. But unless a given group has had experience at catering a horse event, a large show is not the place to experiment. When engaging anyone (or a group) to handle this part of the show operation, the committee in charge should look carefully at his (or its) previous experience and record. There should be no excuse for poor food or poor service.

Commercial booths, other than food and refreshments, usually pay a fixed fee to set up a display at the affair. Those that actually conduct sales of tack or products may be asked to give a percentage of their gross. The concession committee has the job of placing the booths in locations that will not interfere with the show operation, at the same time giving them the best possible exposure.

Stable Management

The subcommittee on stable management has charge of facilities for the care and safety of horses that are kept on the grounds during the event. It sees that box and tie stalls are clean and ready for occupancy, and makes the assignments. It makes arrangements for feed, bedding, water, horse trailer parking, and tack rooms. Every stall must be inspected prior to use and needed repairs should be made before the arrival of the exhibitors and their horses.

In cases where there is no stabling available at the grounds, this committee may scout around the area for possible stall space at private farms or ranches. It investigates the possible use of portable stalls and paddocks that can be rented and set up for the occasion. This must be considered if there is not sufficient space in the existing facilities.

The committee provides for a location of the blacksmith and knows where the veterinarian can be found in case of emergency. It will have direct communication with the show office, day and night, and should have someone present at its own headquarters at all times.

Any event or affair that will require the same horses to be shown on more than one day should provide some kind of stabling for them. At small one-day shows, horses not being in the arena or being ridden are kept at the trailer. Hence, stabling is not necessary, but tie stalls, if present, may be used.

In this day and age when many exhibitors travel with truck campers towing horse trailers, or with combination horse and living trailers, an area must be prepared to take care of these. They will need water, electricity, and sanitary facilities available.

One of the main responsibilities of this committee is that of fire protection in the stabling area. It should set up night patrols just for this purpose and should know the location of all fire fighting equipment.

First Aid

No matter how small or how large a show might be, some arrangement must be made to take care of any medical emergency. Large affairs will set up a regular first aid station with a doctor present and a fully equipped ambulance in attendance. A small one-day show should have at least one person trained in first aid available, along with a station wagon and a stretcher. Even the smallest affair should have several first aid kits handy.

Large shows always take care of the possible medical emergencies, but many one-day events overlook this part of a show operation. They assume nothing of this nature is going to happen during one short day. It is not worth the gamble. At least one person with first aid knowledge should be definitely assigned to the job.

9

Final Preparations

Now that the premium lists and the entry forms are in the mail and all subcommittees are busy at their jobs, it is time to begin the final preparations for the affair.

Program or Catalogue

The program committee has made arrangements with a printer concerning the printing of the catalogue, has determined a deadline for all material needed, and has decided on the number to be run. Certain information can be furnished the printer fairly early: a list of all officials, committees, judges, stewards, acknowledgments and credits, special announcements or pages required by sanctioning associations, schedule of events, and class specifications. Since all advertising needs layout work, it is well to set a deadline for this as well as class sponsors, which must be named for each class. Any time you omit one you have lost a future sponsorship.

As soon after the entries close as possible, the entry secretary must furnish the printer with a list of the exhibitors by number in each class, a list of all exhibitors alphabetically, and a list of all horses by exhibitors' numbers with a description of each.

The timing of getting these lists to the printer is what

usually sets the closing date of entries for an event. For
large affairs with many entries this date may be as much
as four weeks before the actual event itself. For a small
two- or three-day show it may be as little as ten days
prior.

If the program has been turned over to a professional,
he will still need all the above information and he will
set the deadlines for its receipt. For obvious reasons these
must be adhered to strictly.

Some smaller affairs will make up a program containing all of the above information except the list of exhibitors and their horses. However, as soon as this is available, the committee will have the list printed on a separate
sheet to be used as an insert in the program. This may
be done when the list will not exceed one printed page
or a folded sheet that can be inserted in the program.

Many sanctioning associations require a marked program showing the results in each class. Hence great care
must be taken in proofreading, especially the names of
both the exhibitors and the horses.

Programs or catalogues will vary depending on the size
and scope of the affair. Many small one-day affairs will
not go to the trouble of having one but will use the prize
list instead. However, large shows will always put out a
program, its elaborateness depending on the amount of
advertising and the expected sales.

Insurance

This is a must for any event. Public liability insurance
will be necessary for even the smallest of affairs. For a
group or individual that is putting on a show for the first
time, there are several avenues of approach. One is to
investigate through a local insurance agent. Some sanctioning associations have access to coverage for shows

with which they are involved. Their rule books will state this and what must be done to obtain the coverage. For events that have been held before, their records should furnish past information. These should be checked to see if the coverage was sufficient and the costs reasonable.

Clubs and groups, even the unincorporated, should carry liability insurance the year around for any affairs they hold. However, the policy may need a rider to cover the owner of the grounds where the affair is being held. This is one of the requisites in any rented or leased grounds. The owner will insist on being covered by adequate liability insurance.

Organizations that own their grounds, arenas, or show facilities will usually carry various types of insurance on their property, and this should include public liability. It is well to check the policies to make certain any event to which the public is invited is adequately covered.

One member of the show committee, most often the manager, takes care of the insurance. And he should take the time to instruct all committee members on just what is covered and what to do when an insurance question arises.

Police and Fire Protection

Large shows extending over several days will make arrangements for police protection around the clock. If the show is being held at a publicly owned facility, the local police will consider it part of its duty to provide this service. If it is held on semiprivate or private grounds, then some arrangement must be made for the cost of the protection.

In many areas of the country, reserve deputy sheriffs and police are also horsemen, and are even formed into horsemen's groups. They may be asked to provide this protection, either voluntarily or for a donation to their group treasury, depending on the affair's beneficiary.

Even a small one-day event may desire to have police protection, especially where there will be public attendance. Tack and equipment have a way of disappearing, and the presence of a uniformed guard can act as a deterrent.

Fire protection operates along the same lines as police protection. Grounds that are publicly owned will almost always have a sufficient fire protection setup. But regardless of whether the grounds are publicly or privately owned, the manager should check on what fire protection is at hand and what is available.

At any affair where horses are bedded overnight in stalls, there should be a watchman patrol set up both day and night, especially the latter. This patrol should know the location of all fire equipment, alarm boxes, and phones, and should be instructed what to do in case of fire. Nothing will hurt a show more than a stable fire.

Secretarial Work

Once the premium lists and entry forms are in the mail, the entry secretary's work really begins. He or she must be prepared to receive the incoming entries, extract the information contained, enter it on certain forms, and file the entry blanks in a logical fashion. In large affairs and as may be required by a sanctioning association, the receipt of entries must be acknowledged, usually by postcard.

There are several methods of filing the entry forms. The most common way is to place them alphabetically in a looseleaf notebook. Another method is to put them in a box file. Small one-day affairs need only a method where they can be at hand end easily referred to.

There should be a loose-leaf book prepared with all

the classes arranged in numerical order, and possibly another arranged alphabetically, for handy reference. For large affairs with many classes several or more notebooks will be necessary.

Each entry blank should have all the pertinent information taken from it when it is received and before it is filed. Each horse is given a number to use for the duration of the show or event. That number, the name of the horse, the name of the rider, and the name of the owner are placed in the classes indicated in the class notebook. They are also placed on a list in the same numerical order, and entered in the alphabetical file according to name of the owner.

The entry fee is checked against the classes entered and the amount received. Should insufficient payment or overpayment (or lack of payment) be noted, a separate list of such discrepancies should be prepared, and a note attached to the entry blank. These differences will have to be corrected before the contestant will be allowed to show. Usually they are brought to his attention at the time he arrives at the affair.

In the case of events taking several days where stabling will be needed, the entry form will contain a request for same. This must be noted on a stabling sheet, a copy of which will be furnished to the stabling committee. That committee will in turn give the assigned stall number or location to the secretary for the exhibitor's information.

About three days at the most, after the closing date of the entries, all of them should have been received. If the affair is having a program or catalogue made up, then the secretary will need to get a list of the entries to the program committee. It should be in the form decided upon and ready for the printer. There are several forms to use; those arranged alphabetically by owner or exhibitor, numerically by animal, or both. There are samples in the Appendix showing ways it is done.

Now the work sheets may be made up. These are made in the form given in the Appendix. They give the class number and name, the list of exhibitors in that class by number, name of horse, rider, and owner. There will be a column for the award given, and a place for the judge's signature if needed. Copies of the work sheet for each class will go to the ring clerk, the announcer, the back gate man, and the ring steward.

Next is the preparation of the judge's cards. These cards come in various forms, most of which may be purchased commercially from printers who advertise in horse publications. If samples are available a local printer can copy them. Some associations that sanction affairs furnish judge's cards or forms that they want used. At the top of the card or sheet is a space for the class number, name, and the exact specifications of the class. Then near the top are the spaces for the judge to enter his class placings —first, second, etc. In the column on the left, the exhibitors' numbers are entered. In some large shows where the classes are very big and the numbers would cover more than one card or sheet, these are omitted. The judge will use the form to make notes and will enter his placings in the spaces provided. At the bottom of the card or form is a space for the judge's signature.

It is up to the secretary to see that the exhibitors' numbers are on hand. There are two types—the arm band and the back number. These can be either heavy cardboard or a permanent plastic. Almost any saddle shop will be able to order numbers for an affair from the manufacturers' catalogues on hand. Some makers advertise in the

various horse magazines. And there are some feed manufacturers who will furnish numbers free to shows. Since
permanent numbers cost quite a bit and may be used
from year to year, it is customary for some affairs to
require a deposit for them, to be returned to the exhibitor
when he turns his number back to the secretary. This
assures the return of most of the numbers and will pay
for the replacement of those lost.

The secretary prepares the exhibitors' envelopes that
are used at the larger shows or events. These envelopes
should contain the exhibitor's number, a show schedule,
identification badges for the family, grooms, attendants,
meal tickets, parking stickers, stall and tack room assignments, and anything else that will help the contestant.

These can be the large manila envelopes—9 x 12 inches
—that when made up can be filed alphabetically, to be
picked up at the entry secretary's office or booth when
the contestant arrives. Any difference between what the
exhibitor has paid and what his entry shows he owes
should be noted on the outside of the envelope so it can
be called to his attention when he picks it up.

Small affairs do not use the envelope system, but have
the numbers available at the entry booth, using a check-
off list of the entries received. Any discrepancies are
noted on the list and are taken care of when the numbers are given out.

Any changes in the schedule or in any classes that have
not been sent to the entrants must be given to them when
they pick up their numbers or envelopes. The rules of
the various associations will tell the show management
what to do in case of any changes or cancellations of
classes. An alert entry secretary will be aware of these
rules and be prepared to act accordingly.

10

The Show Itself

Now we come to the actual operation of the show or affair itself. An exhibitor first heads for the horse show office or the place he or she will pick up his number, along with the envelope containing the information he needs. This office should be conveniently located, more for the contestant than the management. At large affairs where stabling is provided it will be close to the stall area. At small events, such as a one- or two-day affair, it will be in the vicinity of the announcer's stand or near the center of activity.

All of the entry forms, no matter how filed, must be at this location so that they may be shown to a contestant who has any question. The notebooks containing the entries by class are kept here, and when the class results are turned in to the secretary, they are entered in these books. Judges' cards and the ring clerk's work sheets are turned in to the secretary's office after the awards are announced and presented for a class, and these are kept on file during the affair so that they may be referred to in case of any dispute or question.

Any information, such as class changes or class schedules, is given to the exhibitors as they arrive, even if it has been mailed or called to them previously. This acts as a check and assures there will be no mixup.

If the affair or event is taking post entries, these are handled at the secretary's office or booth. As we have said before, large events that put out a printed program will very seldom take post entries—almost never. However, small one- or two-day shows will, especially if there are other shows going on in the vicinity that might attract the same anticipated exhibitors. In this case, the secretary must be prepared with blank entry forms, money to make change, means of rapid communication with the ring clerks, back gate men and ring stewards, and files in which to make the post entries. For an affair taking post entries to run smoothly, there must be excellent timing and coordination. Some events do very well with post entries; others have difficulty. In any case, experience will tell.

The announcer's booth may be a small spot with room for the announcer and a ring clerk, or it may be a large area with several announcers and clerks. For large events, if the ribbons and trophies are not in the announcer's booth, they should be very close by and ready to be awarded at the end of the class. For small one-day affairs, all the ribbons and trophies for the show may be placed in or near the booth.

The announcer should have one of the copies of the class work sheets, along with a rule book of the association under which the show is being held. He must also have a schedule of events and a copy of the catalogue. If there are class sponsors whose names have been accidentally omitted from the catalogue, the announcer must be told so he can give them the necessary recognition.

Every show that puts out a published catalogue should

have someone designated to mark copies—usually two or three—which become the master catalogues from which others may be marked. Some associations require a marked catalogue to be sent to them with the show results. This marking can be done right at the announcer's booth. However, for any show running over two days, it is best to mark catalogues from the results as shown on the judges' cards, since these are turned into the show office after each session of the affair.

Many shows like to have music during the running of the show, but not many can afford a live orchestra. Hence they will hook up a record table or a tape recorder into the public address system. The best person to control the incidental music is the announcer, even if someone else actually handles the tapes. This is because he knows when such music will not interfere with the performance in the ring.

The ring clerk, who has been given all the work sheets and judges' cards for each performance in the session ahead of time, is prepared to give one work sheet to the announcer, one to the ring steward, and to keep one herself. She also gives the judge's cards to the ring steward, who in turn gives it to the judge. As soon as the judge's card is filled out, signed, and returned to her she can either mark the announcer's work sheet with the results, or let him do it himself. Most announcers prefer to have the work sheet marked before giving the results of the class to the public. There is less chance for error than there is in trying to read off the numbers on the judge's card and transferring them directly to the public address system.

The person in charge of the ribbons and trophies sets up the awards in the order they will be given out. He or she also makes sure that the class sponsor or his representative is present at the right time to hand out the awards. If the class has no sponsor, then the awards chairman tries to line up people to make the presentations, usually important persons or those who may deserve special recognition.

At some events where there is stake money involved and checks are to be given out with the ribbons, it may be necessary for the treasurer to be present to write them out when the results are known. However, if the checks can be made out ahead of time (except for the name of the winning party), it is much better. Then all that must be filled in is the name, and this can be obtained from the work sheet. Checks made out to cash should be avoided if at all possible, since a lost or misplaced check will cause all sorts of problems.

Large shows, especially those at which there are many stake events, usually mail the prize money to the winners after the close of the affair. This way every class may be doubly checked and the chance for error is further eliminated. This method is used mainly at shows that are subsidized, such as fairs and expositions.

The awards chairman should make the arrangements for the presentation of any special prizes, such as challenge cups or annual awards. If possible the original donor or relative should be gotten in touch with for such awards. If not, a previous winner or the like might be asked. In any event, special awards should be handled so that there is no confusion when they are due to be presented.

The judge's place is in the arena, except when not working a class. He should have a chair in the vicinity of the announcer's area, preferably where he can be protected from close contact with exhibitors and spectators. When he is actually judging a class, all he should need is the judge's card, which has been given to him by the ring steward. When the class is over, and the judge has marked his card with the results as he saw them and signed the card, he gives it to the ring steward, who then takes it to the ring clerk. She then gives him the work sheet and judge's card for the next class.

The show stewards are representatives of the sanctioning association. They stay where they can watch the arenas or classes to which they are assigned. At the same time they let the show management and the announcer know where they will be located. This is because they must be available at any time to anyone connected with the affair—judges, exhibitors, and management.

11

Conduct of the Show

If everything has been taken care of properly to this point, and the show is running on schedule, it is time to call the first class. In fact a warning call should have gone out at least ten minutes before the scheduled time. The in gate man has been furnished copies of the work sheets for each class in that session, and now he checks off each contestant as he or she enters the arena. In some classes where all exhibitors compete at the same time, the in gate man merely checks them off as they enter with no regard to the order on his work sheet. If he finds he has some entries missing, he notifies the announcer of their numbers. The announcer then calls for the missing entries over the public address system, giving them a certain amount of time to report to the in gate, not to exceed three minutes. If they have not reported by then, they are considered absent from that class. At small shows, the management will do its best to see that all contestants get into the ring. However, at a large affair, running on a tight schedule, the burden is on the exhibitor to be at his class when it is called.

Because of scratched horses, absent entries, post entries, etc., there must be reliable communication among

73

the entry booth, the announcer's booth, and the in gate man. There is nothing more disconcerting to the in gate man than a contestant who tells him that he is a post entry, but about whom the in gate man has had no knowledge. He will then hold up everything until he can check with either the entry or announcer's booth for verification. The same goes for a ring steward who finds an entry in the arena that is not on his work sheet.

If the class is one in which each contestant performs separately, such as a hunter or jumper class, the in gate man will have a copy of the jumping order, and will have it posted on a blackboard or card so it is visible to a mounted rider. He then makes sure he has the next entry ready to go as soon as the performing contestant leaves the ring. In a large class a good in gate man can speed up a show by having entries ready to go as soon as they are called.

In a class where all contestants are being judged at the same time, the ring steward or ringmaster double checks the number of exhibitors against the number he should have according to his work sheet. In some shows he may even leave this up to the in gate man, who has notified the announcer that all entries are present. In this case the announcer will tell the judge that the class is ready to be judged. If the ring steward has checked his sheet and found the class all present, he then can tell the judge that the class is ready.

The judge observes the class, asking the ringmaster or steward to communicate the judge's wishes, such as a change of gaits, to the announcer. The ringmaster and the announcer should get together on a set of signals that can be easily seen and interpreted. At some large shows with big arenas, the communication may be by walkie-talkie radio. This is very handy when the judge asks for a movement or an individual performance that has not been covered by the prearranged signals. A good ring steward or ringmaster stays within hearing distance of the judge, but tries not to block his view of the contestants. And he talks to the judge only in response to questions and requests.

If it is a jumper or hunter class, or a trail class requiring the contestant to follow a set course, the ringmaster explains the course to the judge and helps the judge check it to see if it conforms to the specifications of the class.

In jumper classes where faults at each jump are scored separately, the judge must have an assistant observer or scorer who watches the obstacles that would be difficult for the judge to cover. Also the judge must have a secretary who writes down the faults as he calls them.

In addition to relaying the judge's instructions, the announcer may give some of the details of the specifications of the class, or direct the incidental music. However, he must be alert to quickly relay the judge's request to the contestants. In jumping classes, he has a copy of the jumping order, and calls the exhibitors into the ring in proper order. If there should be any change in this order, the in gate man should tell the announcer in time for him to make the correction on his work sheet, or his jumping order sheet.

The judge has been sent a copy of the premium list with all the class specifications, and he has prepared himself to judge each class accordingly. He will check the specifications on his judge's card to make sure that there has been no change. If there has, he is governed by what his card will say, governed by the knowledge that any

change from the original will have been furnished the
entrants involved.

After he has finished adjudicating the class, the judge
marks his card with the results. The prize list states to
which place ribbons will be awarded, and he places his
class accordingly. Then he signs the card and gives it
to the ring steward or ringmaster. The latter then hustles
it to the ring secretary as fast as possible. She should
have the new work sheet and judge's card ready to hand
the ring steward in exchange.

The ring secretary now marks her work sheet or the
announcer's work sheet with the results. As noted before, some announcers like to mark their own, in which
case she will hand the judge's card to him to use.

As soon as the announcer has the numbers, name of
rider, horse, and owner, and placings, he then is ready to
announce the awards. He will introduce the sponsor, or
the person giving out the awards, and then call the
placing. He will allow enough time for the person hand-
ing out the trophy and ribbons to make the award, and
if there is a photographer present, to have a picture
taken. All large affairs and many of the smaller ones will
have an official photographer who will take a picture
of the winner and the donor.

As soon as the awards are given out, the announcer
is ready to call for the next class. The ring clerk then
clips the work sheet with the results to the judge's card,
to be turned in to the show secretary after that session.
If it is a one-day affair, she may keep them until the end
of the show.

The above is the general procedure of each class as
it comes along. Some classes, such as hunter or jumper
classes, will require the services of the ring crew. While

the ring is being prepared, the announcer will make spot announcements concerning anything of interest, such as food concessions and coming events, and of course provide music to relieve any monotony.

12

How to Handle a Protest

No matter how sportsmanlike the exhibitors may be, no matter how excellent the management may be, and no matter how knowledgeable the judges may be, there are times when one of them believes that something is wrong. It may be a violation of the rules under which the affair is being conducted; it may be a mistake in the actions of one of the show officials; or it may be one of several things. But in any event it brings a protest or charge. This is something that the show committee must be prepared to handle.

A protest is made by an exhibitor or his agent, or parent in case of a junior. A charge is made by a show official or an officer in the association under whose rules the affair is held.

Each sanctioning association has rules and regulations regarding the handling of protests or charges. These will be found in the respective rule books. Many small one- or two-day affairs are held without a particular sanction, although the prize list and entry form will state that the affair is being held under the rules of one of the various associations. In some cases the prize list will not say whose rules are being used, leaving the entrant to assume which rules are to hold. Since the most comprehensive set of horse show rules is published by the American Horse Shows Association, these are the most referred to, and in case of doubt, the most likely to be adhered to. It is to the management of the smaller shows, not having a sanction, that the following paragraphs are directed.

For an unsanctioned affair, there is no higher echelon to which to turn. The management will have to take care of any protest or charge itself, and cannot pass it up the ladder for a decision by some higher authority. Most protests coming from the exhibitors will be against the judge for failing to follow the specifications for a class, or in the absence of full specifications—the usual practice for such classes. Then again, the protest may be against the management for an alleged violation of the accepted rules. Once in awhile, one exhibitor will make a protest against another, such as the eligibility of his horse for a certain class, or the rider for a class. Allegations such as these must be ironed out as soon as possible. Since the exhibitors are the backbone of any horse event, their complaints must be taken care of to their satisfaction, or at least to the best satisfaction possible under the circumstances.

This means that the management must listen to the complaint, investigate it, and rectify the error—if there is one. If no error has been committed, as far as the management can tell, the complainant must be told why. If he feels that he is being given the brush-off he will be quite unhappy and will convey this unhappiness to everyone within earshot, not only at the show itself, but for a long time afterward. And an irritated exhibitor is one of the worst advertisements that a show can have.

In some small affairs, the show manager is the one to

whom all complaints are directed, no matter what they may be. If he is to do a good job, he must be patient and tactful, and have the wisdom of Solomon. It would be better if he had a committee of at least three people to take care of any protests, someone other than himself or the show secretary. One of the committee should be well-experienced in the working of shows and the classes involved in the particular affair.

There are some things that are not protestable. One of these is a judge's decision, based on his personal preference, unless it was arrived at in violation of the rules or the specifications for the class. Another is a judge's or veterinarian's decision concerning lameness or soundness of a horse. Remember, the judge is making his selection based on his own preference, and no two judges will see the same horses and contestants in exactly the same fashion. A judge with a poor eye for a good performance will not get very many assignments as his reputation spreads. But no matter how he ties his ribbons, his decisions cannot be protested unless they are in error of a rule violation.

If the event has a steward, he will be representing management, exhibitors, judges, and the association under whose rules the affair is being held. Before any formal protest or charge is made, the complaint should be aired to the steward. He will investigate the complaint and try to head off any formal protest. Many times he will find that it is a case of misunderstanding or some other matter that can be taken care of without causing any undue commotion. A steward has no authority in the management or the judging. He is there to help and to act as a buffer. He is the person to whom an exhibitor goes for answers to any questions about rules, anything in the show management that he does not understand, or the conduct of a class in which he is in doubt. As stated earlier, a good steward is invaluable to the management of any equine affair, since he will keep the exhibitors off management's back. Many an affair, without a steward, has found itself embroiled in an ill-advised protest that could have been avoided if a steward had been present.

13

After the Show

It would be nice, once the show or affair is over, to just relax and look forward to the next one—especially someone else's. However, whether it is the only show that group will ever have or just one of a series there are certain details that the management must take care of as soon after the show as possible. Everything will still be fresh in the minds of all the committee chairmen and there are certain requirements of the various sanctioning associations which have deadlines.

The secretary must send either a marked program showing the results of each class, or a separate sheet with the class results on it. Some associations have forms that must be filled out and returned. Here again, the secretary should have read the rules of each of the sanctioning groups and made a check list of what is needed to be done after the show is over. An omission of any requirement is grounds for refusing further sanctions from that particular association.

Another duty of the secretary is to bring the mailing list up to date, noting especially address changes and the names of new exhibitors. If the group has its own mailing list, this can be done at leisure, before it is needed again. However if the group is using someone else's list, such as that of a sanctioning group, the show secretary should pass these changes on to the keeper of the list.

All entry blanks, all judge's cards with results, and all information concerning each class or event should be kept and filed for at least a year. There are many times when one of the sanctioning groups will want to clarify the results of a class, especially when it involves points to be awarded to competitors within that sanctioning group. Having the records handy for referral is quite a help.

The treasurer has the job of paying all the final bills and preparing a financial statement of the show. It is the task of all members of the committee to see that all bills —even the smallest—are immediately passed on to the treasurer for payment. There is nothing so disconcerting as to have closed the books, only to have some small bill come up. If the secretary has kept her entries correctly, along with her record of entry payments, the treasurer should have no difficulty in balancing the income statement of his accounts. But he needs copies of all charges against the show along with his receipts and cancelled checks to satisfy any audit of his books that may be required.

Each committee chairman has the responsibility of returning any rented or borrowed equipment that his committee has used. He also has the responsibility of seeing that equipment belonging to the show or event is stored. This may require checking with the show manager or show chairman as to any storage arrangements. An inventory of all stored equipment should be made and turned into the show secretary to be kept with the permanent show records for use by the next show committee.

A short time following the affair, the show or event

chairman should call a meeting of his committee. Any lessons learned or mistakes made should be gone over for future reference. Exhibitor acceptance and spectator attendance should be checked and reasons found why they were either good or poor. All aspects of the affair should be gone over with the idea of suggesting improvements to future committees.

If a similar affair is planned for the following year, the outgoing committee should recommend the dates and contact the various sanctioning associations for show and date approval. The dates are usually tentative and will be verified within a certain time prior to next year's affair. But it should be the present committee that starts the ball rolling.

Other than the dry records of an event or show, such as program, judges' cards, old work sheets, etc., there is very seldom a written record of what was done, who did it, and how it was done. If each committee chairman would make a brief written report of just what he did, and the show officers did likewise, the information could be gathered in a notebook for the use of future committees. Many times an entirely new group is called on to take over. A guide to go by would be a wonderful help. If this suggestion is made at one of the first committee meetings, long before the final event, there is a chance that some of the committee chairmen may do it. The closer to show time, the harder it is to get anyone to write about what he is doing. He is more interested in getting it done than writing about it. But if he has kept notes, then shortly after the affair it will not be too hard for him to make a written record of his particular position. And anything that will help future committee members from repeating past mistakes—anything that can smooth the work—is always welcome.

14

Combined Training Events

A combined training event consists of two or three of the following: dressage, competition in the open, and jumping. The dressage phase shows the degree of development of the horse and the ability of the rider to execute certain simple movements. The competition in the open shows the ability of the horse and rider to cover varying types of ground, either with or without jumps. The jumping phase shows the ability of the horse and rider to get around a moderate jumping course.

Combined training events, also known as three-day events, were an outcome of competition in the military to show the best trained mount for all around military purposes. The dressage showed the training of the horse in control; the competition in the open showed the ability of the horse and rider to get across country in good shape; and the jumping showed that after the cross-country, the horse was still in good shape, supple and able to negotiate a fair jumping course.

The top three-day event is held at the Olympic Games, in which different countries enter a team. The first three-day Olympic competition was held in 1912 at Stockholm, Sweden, with the winner being Sweden.

There are some special considerations to take into account in planning a combined training event: the availability of an area of sufficient size for dressage and an area long and varied enough for cross-country, and someone in the group with experience with a three-day event. Before looking into these matters, it is well to make sure that there are enough exhibitors interested in attending such an event to make it feasible. It does not take too many to make a successful affair, unlike a horse show. In fact, any more than 50 will cause a problem in time. Even with that many you will be looking at approximately seven hours of dressage.

Since a combined training event may be held with only two of the phases, it is possible to have one with dressage and one with jumping. If there are several three-day events scheduled in an area it may be well to consider a two-phase affair, which might attract exhibitors who do not feel up to a full-scale event.

There are two organizations that publish pamphlets on combined training—the United States Combined Training Association and the American Horse Shows Association. The latter also has available the rules of the Federation Equestre Internationale (F.E.I.), the governing body of all international competition. It is not advisable to consider any combined training event without these rules and pamphlets on hand.

15

Dressage Competitions

Dressage competitions require an arena of a special size and a specialized judge. These competitions are held to show the ability of the horse and the rider to execute a given ride in which the movements will illustrate their degree of training. At the lowest levels it is the rider who is being judged; at the higher levels more emphasis is put on the horse and less on the rider.

The lowest level is Pony Club D, and the highest is F.E.I. level for international competition. There are many levels in between. As one progresses up the ladder the movements required of the horse become more difficult and complicated, all pointed to show the degree of training, and the willingness and the response to the rider, without resistance.

There are two ring sizes that may be used: 20 meters by 40 meters (66 feet by 132 feet), and 20 meters by 60 meters (66 feet by 198 feet). The smaller may be used for levels up to and including Level Two. The larger arena is the official size and must be used at all levels above Level Two, but may also be used for Levels One and Two. The arena should have a fence around it, not higher than 16 inches, with a movable section at the far end, away from the judge, about 13 feet or so in length. In Appendix K is a diagram of the two arenas, with the lettering used to indicate marking points for the movements. The markers should be large enough to be easily read from any point in the arena, on the outside of the fence, yet close enough to the latter so as to definitely mark a point of change.

The jury, which may be one or more judges, not only judges but also makes remarks on the judging sheet that will tell the rider his and his horse's weak points, their strong points, and the general impression of the rider. Hence, dressage judges are people with the special understanding necessary not only to grade the movements, but also to make comments on them. Therefore a show committee, in selecting one or more judges, must be extremely careful to choose either an accredited person, or one with the necessary knowledge.

One of the key things to keep in mind when considering a dressage competition is the amount of time involved in each scheduled ride. From the Pony Club D, which take about five to six minutes to the high levels which will take up to ten minutes, the more riders there are the longer the show will run. If two arenas are available, it may be well to engage more than one judge and hold the lower levels in one arena under one judge and the higher levels in the other ring under another judge.

Once the entries to a dressage event are closed, it is best to set up a schedule to that each rider will know when he is due in the arena. This can be done by knowing the length of a required ride and adding several minutes on to it for the judge to check over his sheet, and allowing that much time for each competitor. Then a time schedule is drawn and furnished each rider. A class with 30 riders may take as long as five hours and there is no reason for a rider who has drawn a later time to be ready when the first rider is due to enter the arena.

Again, the American Horse Shows Association, the United States Combined Training Association, and the United States Pony Clubs all have literature on dressage competitions. In addition, there are a number of dressage societies active throughout the country.

16

Gymkhana

Gymkhana originally meant "games on horseback." The word originated in India when the British cavalry units were stationed there. The British developed games, some of which were already practiced by the native Indian horsemen, and timed events that were held to foster horsemanship among the officers and the native cavalrymen.

Over the years gymkhana has developed into a group of timed events, such as pole bending, barrel racing, numerous types of stake racing, and ring spearing. A gymkhana show will include different events that will be broken down into classes determined by age of rider, size of horse, experience of either or both, and other ways of equalizing the competition.

There are several things to consider when thinking about a gymkhana affair. First, a judge who thoroughly knows the rules under which the show will be held is necessary. Second, an arena large enough is needed. It must be at least 120 feet by 200 feet, with good footing. Third, a method of timing is necessary. Electric timing is preferred, but hand timers may be used. However, even with electric timers, a manually operated stop watch must be used as a back-up. Fourth, special equipment such as poles, stakes, and barrels is a must. These should be to the specifications of the rules under which the affair is being held.

There are almost as many different sets of rules for gymkhana as there are riders. However, the American Horse Shows Association has adopted a Gymkhana Division and is developing a set of rules for certain events. As time goes on, more will be added. In the meantime, AHSA does publish a pamphlet *Suggestions for Gymkhana Events*. The American Quarter Horse Association includes rules for some events in its rule book. Some state associations, such as the California State Horsemen's Association, publish a rather comprehensive rule book covering just about all gymkhana events.

17

Hunter Trials

Hunter trials are just what the name implies—a competition of hunters over courses designed to best show the ability of the horse to follow hounds over varied terrain and varied types of jumps normally found on the hunting grounds.

In addition to an arena, there is needed an outside course of sufficient length to show the horse's pace and manners along with its jumping ability. A good outside course will have anywhere from 10 to 20 fixed and permanent jumps, representing what might be found on an actual hunt. These are usually fences, walls, ditches, water, brush, banks, coops, gates, etc. They will vary in height and spread, depending on the degree and the type of competitor.

In deciding what course to lay out and what jumps to use, the committee must take into account the ability of the anticipated exhibitors. Good hunter trials will have classes for all degrees of competition, from pony hunters and first-year green horses up to the top hunters that are experienced and have hunted regularly. Team classes are very popular, with teams coming from various hunts or clubs. Also quite popular are in hand classes for breeding stock, yearlings, two-year olds, etc., where the animals are shown with halter.

Hunter trials are usually fun affairs with classes for all hunting type horses and would-be hunters. There might be children's classes for pony hunters, ladies' classes, classes for side-saddle, classes restricted to riders from certain areas or with certain qualifications, such as members of a given hunt. Only the imagination of the trials committee will limit the number and kinds of events that may be held.

18

Competitive Trail Riding

Trail riding competition breaks down into two categories: competitive trail riding and endurance riding. The former is controlled by time, with emphasis on the condition and soundness of the horse; the latter is strictly against time, with certain consideration being given to soundness and condition, as determined at given check points. There is a third type of competition that is usually held in conjunction with pleasure rides, taking place over a period of three days to a week. On rides like these, awards are given to the best trail horse, best senior or junior rider, and best sportsman; there is a horsemastership award for best care of the horse, and other similar awards.

There are many good trail rides throughout the country that have been held annually over the years. Before 1961, each of the competitive type were held without regard to others. There was no association among them and there was no annual award in the different categories. In that year a group representing several different rides got together and formed the North American Trail Ride Conference. This group pooled its knowledge to help one another, and to sanction rides in which winners would receive points toward annual awards. This group now covers most of the western states and has grown steadily through the years.

Endurance rides have been held for years. One of the oldest and best known is the Green Mountain Ride, held annually in Vermont. Another is the Tevis Cup Ride, a 100-miler held each summer in the Sierras. These rides are primarily against time, with a number of check points where a team of veterinarians go over each horse to determine if he is fit to continue on the ride.

Competitive trail riding is usually a one- or two-day affair, taking place in rolling or mountainous country over a route about 40 miles per day. Since the time of the ride is controlled, before the event some experienced horseman must have ridden the route on a well-conditioned horse in order to determine time needed by a normal horse and rider to complete the distance. It may be that one can get over the whole route by car or jeep and by this find out the exact distance, but this will not take the place of an actual rider checking it out.

For affairs such as these two judges are needed, one a lay horseman, and the other a veterinarian. The two work in conjunction with each other, determining condition, soundness, and manners. In the case where there is a large group of novice division, it may be necessary to have another similar pair of judges. On most rides it is not feasible for the judges to go along on horseback. They should be put in selected spots so as to observe the whole ride from these vantage points. They cannot do this if riding on horses.

Veterinary science has discovered a relationship between pulse and respiration and recovery rate after exercise in determining the condition of a horse. Experience has shown that a number of teams of three can do the job for the judges, furnishing them the figures. One takes pulse, one respiration, and one records. Since there is a definite time involved, the number of teams will depend on the number of riders. A good team can check a horse in a little less than a minute, and the same horse should be checked again in exactly ten minutes. It must be the same for all horses or the results will be distorted.

On a competitive ride, stabling, feeding, and taking care of the competitors' needs are very important. Another very important aspect is communications. In many instances, local ham radio clubs will volunteer their services if contacted. Also, a stand-by horse trailer is needed to pick up animals who have had to quit the ride because of poor condition or accident. Management has many details to care for on a competitive ride, the least of which is marking the trail. It has to be thoroughly marked, especially the turns and forks where a wrong move means a lost rider. A small map or sketch of the route with estimated distances and times is a great help to riders who have not been over the ground before.

The North American Trail Ride Conference is preparing three pamphlets on competitive trail riding: one for judges, one for riders, and the other for management. These should be available shortly.

Endurance riding is slightly different. Since time is the key factor, the main function of the judges, usually veterinarians, is to determine the condition of the finishing horse for any special award. The fact that a horse finished the ride without being pulled or held up at any of the check points speaks well for his condition. But there must be enough check points to prevent a rider from overworking his horse to the point of exhaustion, and to check on lameness.

Here again, on endurance rides, someone must have gone over the trail on horseback to make sure there is no insurmountable object. Feeding of horse and rider is only a problem before and after the ride. Communications are still important and some preparation must be made to evacuate either a down horse or rider.

19

Playdays

Playdays are usually small one-day affairs, local in nature, with training classes, various fun classes, and games, mainly for the benefit of junior riders. Playdays may be open to only the members of a certain club or group, or there may be competition between clubs or groups. In all cases, the entry fee is quite nominal, merely to cover expenses.

The appeal of this type of event is to have something for everyone. By carefully examining the nature of the expected contestants as to age, type of horse, and capabilities, one can come up with a varied program that will get everybody into several classes. Games, such as musical chairs and its many variations, and other types that get young riders on and off horses, contribute to a fun-filled day. Gymkhana events, modified to fit the contestants, are always well received. Bareback equitation is a good class for a playday.

Many older people in a club ride for the pleasure of it, but if certain classes are designed to appeal to them, they will enter into the spirit of the affair. Parent classes and family classes are quite popular at playdays. There is nothing Junior likes better than to see his mother or dad on a horse in competition.

20

Jumping Competitions

A show may be made up entirely of jumping classes, although jumping is almost always included as a divison in an all-around affair. Classes for hunters, based on performance, will require jumps of a certain type, such as might be found in natural hunting country. All hunters are expected to jump, but not all jumpers are hunters. There is a definite difference between the two. Hunters are scored on conformation, soundness, and performance, whereas jumpers are scored on performance only. Thus, the design of courses for jumpers will differ greatly from those for hunters.

Jumpers, under the rules of the American Horse Shows Association, are divided into Preliminary, Intermediate, and Open, depending on the amount of money won in stake classes at shows sanctioned by AHSA. Unless prohibited by the show, a horse may compete at a higher level than its classification, but he cannot compete at a lower level.

The design of jumper courses is an art, learned from actual competition, observance, and experience. The designer must have a general idea of the ability of the expected entries in order to plan intelligently. Too many clean performances means too many jump-offs. Although they are crowd pleasers, they are time consuming. On the other hand too difficult courses will make for no clean rounds, with many knock-downs, which also causes delays due to resetting the jumps.

Jumping may be scored on faults, including touches, without regard to time; or on faults, excepting touches, with time as a factor; or on faults only, again excluding touches. A balanced program will have some classes of each type.

In designing courses for junior riders, the planner must keep in mind that in almost every class the maximum height to which the jumps may be raised during jump-offs is five feet. Therefore he will lay out courses where the thinking by the rider and the ability of the horse are stressed. If time is a factor, he will make courses where handiness helps.

What has been said so far applies to large shows; but what of the smaller affairs that would like to schedule some jump classes but nothing elaborate? Some small shows can scrape together only four, five, or six jumps. In Appendix G in this book, there are suggested layouts for jump courses involving four to eight jumps. It is well to remember that no matter how many actual jumps are set up, a competitor should be required to jump eight times, even if he jumps one or more of them twice or more.

When the help needed to move jumps in and out of the arena is scarce, it is well to try to set the jumps up once, leaving them in position for different classes, merely changing directions and heights for various courses. In large arenas, performance classes can be held along the rail without moving any jumps. In smaller rings, the wings nearest the rail may be moved in. In this fashion it is not necessary that all jump classes be held one right after the other, but can be interspersed with performance classes on the rail.

It is not necessary to show a plan of all jumping courses in the prize list. Large affairs almost always do it out of courtesy. Smaller affairs may mail a copy to all jumping class entries. In case the exhibitor has not been furnished copies of the courses, they must be posted at least an hour before the class is to be called. If possible, they should be posted in a conspicuous and convenient place where they can be read from horseback and the rider can see the arena at the same time.

Although many small affairs do not do this, a jumping order should be drawn by lot for each class and posted near the in gate. Care must be taken to allow for an exhibitor showing more than one jumper to have time between his jumps.

Most jumping competitions are held under the rules of the American Horse Shows Association or the Federation Equestre Internationale. These rules are very definite as to the number and types of jumps, heights and spreads for different classes, and scoring. The prize list must state whose rules are being used, and these must be adhered to at the show. Any change in the specifications of a jumping class must be communicated to the contestants concerned as soon as possible. And care must be taken that all involved exhibitors receive the changes.

The American Horse Shows Association publishes a pamphlet, *Planning the Jumper Division,* which contains much valuable information for those responsible for that section of a show. The cost of this is quite nominal and is well worth it. It is recommended for every course planner—experienced or inexperienced.

Appendix

On the following pages examples of various forms are shown. These are guides that can be copied or adapted to the show at hand. There are plans for building different jumps, both movable and fixed. It is hoped that here the management of almost any type of competition will find something useful.

APPENDIX A
PRIZE LISTS

On the next few pages are reproductions of pages from various premium or prize lists. The 1969 premium list for the California State Fair Horse Show took 104 pages, excluding the cover, for a ten-day affair. The prize list for the 1969 California State Horsemen's Association Championship Horse Show, a six-day affair, took 44 pages, not counting the cover. From these we come down to a simple one-day schooling show where all the information, along with the entry form, is on one sheet.

The first page shown is that of the 1969 CSHA prize list. This is the American Horse Shows Association page and is required to be in the prize or premium list of any show that is a member of the association. The rating as stated on the page will vary, depending on the status of the member show and the amount of prize money offered in the different divisions.

Page two lists the show officials and the approvals from certain organizations. Note the closing date on the bottom of the page, along with the statement on post entries. This is thoroughly covered in the general rules and regulations, printed elsewhere in the prize list.

Page three gives the entry fees, where to send them, and other important information, along with the name of the show secretary, her address, and phone number.

Following is page 29 of the California State Fair Horse Show premium list for 1969. It is the first page of the "Index to Classes." The index ran for 10½ pages, covering 402 classes arranged by divisions.

Next is shown the first page of the "Schedule of Events" from the same premium list. As can be seen, it lists the

The California State Horsemen's Association

CHAMPIONSHIP HORSE SHOW

is operated in accordance with the current rules of

THE AMERICAN HORSE SHOWS ASSOCIATION

Rated "A" in Western Pleasure and Western Trail Horse sections. Rated "B" in Green Working Hunter, Regular Working Hunter and Amateur Owner Working Hunter. Rated "C" in all other division and sections.

Every person who participates in the show is responsible for a knowledge of and is subject to the Association Rules. Spectators will better enjoy the show by knowing them. Members receive a copy of the current Rule Book and "Horse Show" and are entitled to participate in the Annual Horse of the Year Award competitions.

No points will be counted toward the Annual Horse of the Year Award Competitions before membership dues have been paid and horses have been recorded with the A.H.S.A.

ANNUAL CONVENTION

Waldorf Astoria - New York, New York

January 14 - 17, 1969

AMERICAN HORSE SHOWS ASSOCIATION, INC.

527 Madison Avenue, New York, N.Y. 10022 TEL. 212-PLaza 9-3070

Albert E. Hart, Jr., President   Walter B. Devereux, Secretary

I hereby apply for . . . . membership and enclose
payment for $. . . . . (Membership expires December 31.)
Life . . . . $250   Senior $15.00
Contributing . . . . $ 25   Junior - under 18 years. . . $ 7.50
Juniors give date and year of birth. . . . . , 19 . . . .
(Dues include $1 for subscription to "Horse Show")
Name . . . .
                              Print Name

Address . . . .
            Street   Route   Box No.

City, State and Zip . . . .

1

California State Horseman's Association
Twenty-Fifth Annual
CHAMPIONSHIP HORSE SHOW
August 18, 19, 20, 21, 22 and 23, 1969
Sonoma County Fairgrounds
Santa Rosa, California

STATE OFFICERS

George M. Dean .... President
Heber James Brown .... Vice-President
Frank J. Connerty .... Vice-President
Harold Swanson .... Vice-President
Fred I. Kemm .... Treasurer
Mrs. Betty Menefee .... Secretary

HORSE SHOW STAFF

John B. Costa .... Chairman-Manager
Mrs. Marie J. Kemm.......................... Secretary
Fred I. Kemm................................. Treasurer

HORSE SHOW JUDGES

Don Burt .... Portuguese Bend, California
Western and Stock Seat Equitation

Richard F. Deller .... Montague, California
Western and Stock Seat Equitation

Eldon J. Fairbanks .... Arcadia, California
Hunters, Jumpers, Hunter Seat Equitation,
Saddle Horses and Welsh Ponies

Col. Earl Thomson .... Santa Barbara, California
Dressage, Hunters, Jumpers, and Hunter Seat Equitation

Frank L. Ely .... Dinuba, California
Gymkhana

A.H.S.A. STEWARDS

Warren M. Underwood .... Santa Barbara, California
Ralph V. Walker .... San Diego, California

SUPERVISOR OF JUMPING COURSES

Col. Alex P. Sysin........................ Elk Grove, California

SUPERVISOR OF TRAIL COURSES

Mrs. Nancy McCall .... San Rafael, California

OFFICIAL PHOTOGRAPHER

June Fallow .... Pittsburg, California

This Championship Horse Show is recognized or approved by these organizations.

American Horse Shows Association - Class "A", "B" and "C"
California Dressage Society
California Reined Cow Horse Association
California State Horsemen's Association as a junior point show
Northern California Chapter of the Professional Horsemen's Association as a junior point show
Pacific Coast Hunter, Jumper and Stock Horse Association - Class "B"

ENTRIES CLOSE JULY 21, 1969 - NO POST ENTRIES

2

INFORMATION

All checks must be made payable to the CALIFORNIA STATE HORSE-MEN'S ASSOCIATION and sent with entry blanks to MRS. MARIE J. KEMM, 30 MARTIN LANE, WOODSIDE, CALIFORNIA 94062. Telephone 415-851-1557 after 6:30 P.M. weekdays. After Thrusday, August 15, call Horse Show Office at Santa Rosa 707-546-4400.

For INFORMATION, PRIZE LISTS AND ADDITIONAL ENTRY BLANKS contact Mrs. Marie J. Kemm.

*   *   *   *

SCHEDULE OF CHARGES
ENTRY FEES

Junior Exhibitor Classes	$ 5.00
Gymkhana, Individual Competitors....................	$ 5.00
Gymkhana, Team, Per Member	$ 5.00
Open Classes, No Prize Money	$ 5.00
Open Classes - Prize Money $ 50.00	$ 10.00
Open Classes - Prize Money $ 75.00	$ 10.00
Open Classes - Prize Money $ 100.00	$ 15.00
Open Classes - Prize Money $ 125.00	$ 15.00
Open Classes - Prize Money $ 150.00	$ 15.00

Silver plate offered in all classes, except when prize money is offered.

*   *   *   *

STALLS

BOX STALLS - Horse, tack or feed -
entire show or lesser period $12.50

First bedding will be provided for each stall. The stabling office will be located in the horse show office building.

*   *   *   *

VACATION TRAILER SPACE

Entire Show .... $ 5.00

*   *   *   *

ENTRIES CLOSE - JULY 21, 1969 - NO POST ENTRIES

1969—116th ANNUAL CALIFORNIA STATE FAIR HORSE SHOW
Sponsored by the 52nd District Agricultural Association

INDEX TO CLASSES

CLASS NO. 1—HACKNEY PONIES
SECTION
1   13 Hands and under .... Sat. Eve., June 7
2   Over 13 hands .... Sun. Eve., June 8
3   $500 Championship Stake .... Sun. Eve., June 15
4   Ladies to drive .... Mon. Eve., June 9
5   Amateur to drive .... Fri. Eve., June 13
6   Gentlemen to drive .... Wed. Eve., June 11

CLASS NO. 2—ROADSTERS
SECTION
7   $500 Wagon Championship Stake Thurs. Eve., June 12
8   $500 Bike Championship Stake .... Sat. Eve., June 14
9   Wagon—Gentlemen to drive ...... Mon. Eve., June 9
10 Bike, Gentlemen to drive .... Sat. Eve., June 7
11 Combination .... Wed. Eve., June 11

CLASS NO. 3—HARNESS PONIES
SECTION
12 $500 Championship Stake .... Sat. Eve., June 14
13 Ladies to drive .... Tues. Eve., June 10
14 Amateur to drive .... Thurs. Eve., June 12
15 Gentlemen to drive .... Sun. Eve., June 8

CLASS NO. 4—FINE HARNESS HORSES
SECTION
16 $500 Championship Stake .... Sun. Eve., June 15
17 Ladies to drive .... Wed. Eve., June 11
18 Amateur to drive .... Sat. Eve., June 7
19 Gentlemen to drive .... Mon. Eve., June 9
20 $500 Junior Stake (Four and under) Fri. Eve. June 13

CLASS NO. 5—FIVE GAITED SADDLE HORSES
SECTION
21 Stallion-Gelding .... Sat. Eve., June 7
22 Mares .... Sun. Eve., June 8
23 $1,00 Championship Stake .... Sun. Eve., June 15
24 Ladies to ride .... Thurs. Eve., June 12
25 $500 Amateur Stake .... Thurs. Eve. June 10
26 Junior (Four and under) .... Mon. Eve., June 9
27 Novice .... Sat. Eve., June 14

CLASS NO. 6—THREE GAITED SADDLE HORSES
SECTION
28 Not exceeding 15.2 Hands .... Sat. Eve., June 7
29 Over 15.2 Hands .... Sun. Eve., June 8
30 $1,000 Championship Stake .... Sat. Eve., June 14
31 Ladies to ride .... Mon. Eve., June 9
32 $500 Amateur Stake .... Wed. Eve., June 11
33 Junior (Four and under) .... Fri. Eve., June 13
34 Novice .... Tue. Eve., June 10

ENTRIES CLOSE MAY 2, 1969

Sponsored by
The 52nd District Agricultural Association

SCHEDULE OF EVENTS

Friday Afternoon, June 6, 1969 — 1:00 P.M.
MAIN ARENA

EVENT	SECTION	
1	39	Conformation Hunters—Handy
2	45	Green Conformation Hunters—Handy—1st Year
3	45-A	Green Conformation Hunters—Handy—2nd Year
4	51	Working Hunters—Handy
5	200	Tenn. Walking Horse Stallions—Three and over
6	201	Tenn. Walking Horse Stallions—Two
7	202	Tenn. Walking Horse Stallions—Yearlings
8	203	CHAMPION AND RESERVE TENN. WALKING HORSE STALLION
9	204	Tenn. Walking Horse Mares—Three and over
10	205	Tenn. Walking Horse Mares—Two
11	206	Tenn. Walking Horse Mares—Yearlings
12	207	CHAMPION AND RESERVE TENN. WALKING HORSE MARE
13	208	Tenn. Walking Horse Geldings—Three and over
14	209	Tenn. Walking Horse Geldings—Two and under
15	210	CHAMPION AND RESERVE TENN. WALKING HORSE GELDING

Saturday Morning, June 7, 1969 — 8:00 A.M.
MAIN ARENA

EVENT	SECTION	
1	38	Conformation Hunters—Amateur
2	44	Green Conformation Hunters—Appointments—1st Yr.
3	44-A	Green Conformation Hunters—Appointments—2nd Yr.
4	50	Working Hunters—Amateur
5	56	Green Working Hunters—Handy—1st Year
6	56-A	Green Working Hunters—Handy—2nd Year
7	360	American Saddlebred Pleasure Three Gaited—Open

Saturday Morning, June 7, 1969 — 8:00 A.M.
OUTSIDE RING

ARABIAN HORSE HALTER DIVISION

EVENT	SECTION	
1	362	Stallions—Four and over
2	363	Stallions—Three
3	364	Stallions—Two
4	365	Stallions—Yearlings
5	366	CHAMPION AND RESEVRE STALLION
6	367	Mares—Four and over
7	368	Mares—Three
8	369	Mares—Two
9	370	Mares—Yearlings
10	371	CHAMPION AND RESERVE MARE
11	372	Geldings—Five and over
12	373	Geldings—Four and under
13	374	CHAMPION AND RESERVE GELDING
14	375	Get of Sire
15	376	Produce of Dam

ENTRIES CLOSE MAY 2, 1969

CYPRESS RING — 2:30 P.M.

1	89	Stock Horses - Riders 14 and under
2	127	Figure Eight Stake Race - Open
3	77	Hunter Seat Equitation - Novice - Riders 12 thru 14

OAK RING — 3:30 P.M.

1	25	Western Trail Horses - Open

Tuesday Evening - August 19, 1969
BECK ARENA — 6:30 P.M.

1	85	Jumper Championship - Riders 17 and under
2	56	A.H.S.A. Hunter Seat Medal Class
3	33	Working Hunters Under Saddle - Open
4	134	Quadrangle Stake Race - Open
5	135	Quadrangle Stake Race - Riders 17 and under

CYPRESS RING — 7:30 P.M.

1	90	Stock Horses - Riders 15 thru 17
2	36	Western Pleasure Horses - Amateur Owner

Wednesday Morning - August 20, 1969
BECK ARENA — 8:30 A.M.

1	122	Working Hunters - Riders 15 thru 17
2	121	Working Hunters - Riders 14 and under
3	61	Bridle Path Hacks - Riders 11 and under
4	62	Bridle Path Hacks - Riders 12 thru 14
5	78	Hunter Seat - Novice - Riders 15 thru 17
6	137	Single Pole Race - Open

CYPRESS RING — 9:30 A.M.

1	60	Ronnie Richards Medal Class - Riders 12 and under
2	98	Stock Seat Equitation - Novice - Riders 11 and under

OAK RING — 11:00 A.M.

1	114	Western Trail Horse Championship - Riders 17 and under

Wednesday Afternoon - August 20, 1969
BECK ARENA — 1:30 P.M.

1	9	Jumpers, Handy - Open - Table I
2	12	Preliminary Jumpers, Handy - Table 2
3	63	Bridle Path Hacks - Riders 15 thru 17
4	66	English Pleasure Horses - Riders 15 thru 17
5	45	Hunter Seat Equitation - Riders 18-21

CYPRESS RING — 1:30 P.M.

1	91	Stock Horse Championship - Riders 17 and under
2	47	Stock Seat Equitation - Riders 18 thru 21
3	138	Two - Man Relay - Open

OAK RING — 3:30 P.M.

1	49	Western Trail Horses - Riders 18 thru 21

CLASS NO. 7—CONFORMATION HUNTERS

HORSES ENTERED IN THIS CLASS ARE NOT ELIGIBLE TO ENTER IN GREEN CONFORMATION, WORKING HUNTERS, WORKING GREEN HUNTERS, AND JUMPERS.

Section 35
Entry Fee $25 $500 CONFORMATION HUNTER OPEN STAKE. To be eligible horses must have been entered, shown and judged in one other performance section over fences, in this class. To be judged on performance, manners and way of going 60%; conformation, quality, substance and soundness 40%; jumps about 4' in height. Full Point Class.

1st	2nd	3rd	4th	5th	6th	7th	8th	9th	10th
$100	85	70	55	45	35	30	30	25	25
Trophy

Section 36
Entry Fee $10 CONFORMATION HUNTERS, SHOWN WITH APPOINTMENTS. To be judged on performance, manners and way of going 60%; conformation, quality, substance and soundness 25%; appointments 15%; jumps about 4' in height. Full Point Class.
Out of each entry fee $5 and divided;
1st, 30%; 2nd, 25%; 3rd, 20%; 4th, 15%; 5th, 10%

1st	2nd	3rd	4th	5th
$45	35	20	15	10
Trophy

Section 37
Entry Fee $10 CONFORMATION HUNTERS RIDDEN BY A LADY. To be judged on performance, manners and way of going 75% with emphasis on manners; conformation, quality, substance and soundness 25%; jumps about 4' in height. Full Point Class.
Out of each entry fee $5 added and divided;
1st, 30%; 2nd, 25%; 3rd, 20%; 4th, 15%; 5th, 10%

1st	2nd	3rd	4th	5th
$45	35	20	15	10
Trophy

Section 38
Entry Fee $10 CONFORMATION HUNTERS RIDDEN BY AN AMATEUR. To be judged on performance, manners and way of going 75%; conformation, quality, substance and soundness 25%; jumps about 4' in height. Full Point Class.
Out of each entry fee $5 added and divided;
1st, 30%; 2nd, 25%; 3rd, 20%; 4th, 15%; 5th, 10%

1st	2nd	3rd	4th	5th
$45	35	20	15	10
Trophy

Section 39
Entry Fee $10 CONFORMATION HANDY HUNTERS. To be judged on performance, manners and way of going 75%; conformation, quality, substance and soundness 25%; jumps about 4' in height. Full Point Class.
Out of each entry fee $5 added and divided;
1st, 30%; 2nd, 25%; 3rd, 20%; 4th, 15%; 5th, 10%

1st	2nd	3rd	4th	5th
$45	35	20	15	10
Trophy

ENTRIES CLOSE MAY 2, 1969

Class 22 — Western Pleasure Horses - Open
Entry Fee $10
> Specifications are the same as Class 21. Prize money $50.00.

Class 23 — Western Pleasure Horses, Sweepstakes - Open
Entry Fee $15
> Specifications are the same as Class 21. To be eligible horses must have been shown, entered and judged in Class 21 or 22. Prize money $100.00.

★　　★　　★　　★

Class 24 — Western Trail Horses, Novice - Open
Entry Fee $10
> To be shown at a walk, jog trot and lope both ways of the ring on a reasonable loose rein without undue restraint. Horses to be shown over and through obstacles. To be judged on performance with emphasis on manners, 60%; appointments, equipment, neatness (silver not to count), 20%; and conformation, 20%. Prize money $75.00.

Class 25 — Western Trail Horses - Open
Entry Fee $15
> Specifications are the same as Class 24. Prize money $125.00.

Class 26 — Western Trail Horses, Sweepstakes - Open
Entry Fee $15
> Specifications are the same as Class 24. To be eligible horses must have been entered, shown and judged in Class 24 or 25. Prize money $150.00.

★　　★　　★　　★

Class 27 — Working Hunter Hacks - Open
Entry Fee $10
> To be shown at a walk, trot and canter both ways of the ring. At least eight horses, if available, are required to jump two fences 3' 6" and gallop one way of the ring. No A.S.H.A. points. Prize money $75.00.

Class 28 — Working Hunter Hacks - Stake - Open
Entry Fee $15
> To be eligible, horses must have been entered, shown and judged in one other class in this section. Specifications are the same as Class 27. No A.S.H.A. points. Prize money $125.00.

Class 29 — Working Hunters - Handy - Open
Entry Fee $10
> To be judged on performance and soundness. Jumps 4'. Full point class. Prize money $50.00.

Class 30 — Working Hunters Shown in Livery
Entry Fee $10
> Riders to wear hunt livery. To be judged on performance and soundness. Jumps 4'. Full Point class. Prize money $50.00.

beginning hour of the first class for each session and the order of the following classes. This index ran for 12½ pages.

Also shown, is page 13 of the 1969 CSHA show's prize list, a page from its "Schedule of Events."

Any show running three days or longer, with 50 or more classes in quite a few divisions, will do well to include both an index and a schedule in its premium list. It is a great help to a prospective exhibitor in figuring what classes he can best enter, considering the timing and the stabling requirements he may need.

Following is a page from the class specification section of the California State Fair Show. In addition to the description of the class, it tells the entry fee and the division of the prize money for the class. Also shown is page 21 of the CSHA list. The same things are listed here except for the breakdown of the prize money. This is given elsewhere in the prize list.

Following is the prize list for a breed show. This was mimeographed on two 8½″ x 11″ sheets, folded once, along with the separate entry blank of the same size, and made for easy mailing. Since it was a breed show—Appaloosa, in this case—certain requirements were carefully spelled out, especially concerning registration.

MAY 31 + JUNE 1, 1969   8:00 A.M.

MID VALLEY APPALOOSA HORSE CLUB
5TH ANNUAL APPALOOSA HORSE SHOW

OAKDALE RODEO GROUNDS	JUDGE
OAKDALE, CALIFORNIA	WM. HOWARD

RULES AND REGULATIONS

Registration

All classes will be governed by the APHC and AHSA rules. APHC papers required for Appaloosas (OPEN CLASSES are open to all breeds). HALTER classes 1 through 24 are APPALOOSA ONLY. CLASSES 25 through 29 are P.O.A. ONLY. PERFORMANCE CLASSES AS STATED. Registration numbers for Appaloosas must accompany entry blank, and *papers must be presented when receiving numbers*. Numbers to be picked up at show grounds at 7:00 A.M. day of show. 1969 Foals need not be registered to show, but must have recognizable Appaloosa markings.

Screening

All Appaloosas must have definite coat markings, and they must be recognizable from at least 12 feet. Two screening committees (one for Appaloosa entries, and one for P.O.A. entries) will be present on the grounds. Any Appaloosa not recognizable from the required distance will be excused, and entry fees will not be refunded. P.O.A. entries will be subject to the P.O.A. rulings and decision of the P.O.A. screening committee.

Protests

All protests will be properly filed, only if accompanied by a deposit of $25.00. Said protest must be filed within 48 hours with the Show Secretary.

Approvals

Mid Valley's show has been approved by the Appaloosa Horse Club, Inc., Moscow, Idaho, Cal-Western Appaloosa, Northern regional Appaloosa Clubs, and is an approved "A" point show for P.O.A.'s. This show is also approved for the Bentley Buckle Award.

Trophies

Trophies will be awarded for all first places, and ribbons will be given to sixth place. Two HIGH POINT PERFORMANCE TROPHIES will be awarded as follows: One Hi-point award will be given to the highest accumulation of points in Classes #37, 41, 46, 48, and 49. The second high-point award will be awarded to the highest accummulation of points in Classes #32, 46, and 44.

Stallions—Who May Show Them

"Performance Classes are open to Stallions, mares, and geldings, with the exception that WOMEN OR CHILDREN MAY NOT RIDE STAL-LIONS IN CLASSES DESIGNATED AS 'WOMEN, LADIES' OR 'CHILDREN, YOUTH OR JUNIOR' (Under 18). STALLIONS MAY BE SHOWN BY ANYONE IN ALL CLASSES IN OTHER DIVI-SIONS." . . . . as quoted by the Appaloosa Show and Contest Manual.

Entries—Fees and Deadline

Entry fees will be $5.00 per class—JUNIORS will have an entry fee of $3.00. Entry deadline is May 22 (entries must be postmarked no later than midnight this day). *Post Entries* will have an additional charge of $2.00 per class entered. No entries will be accepted later than two classes before class entered. All fees to accompany entry blanks. REFUNDS will only be allowed where a certificate of disability or inability to compete is furnished by a duly certified Veterinarian. STALL FEES will be $6.00 per stall for the whole weekend of show time. This fee will include 1 bale of straw.

(Smile!—This is a fun show!)

The management reserves the right to change the sequence of the events on the program and the right to cancel classes if less than three horses entered.

Each rider is allowed only one horse per class in Trail, Barrels, Stump and Stake Race.

STALL SPACE IS LIMITED—Please reserve early.

Classes

HALTER—MAY 31 (Saturday—8:00 AM)
PERFORMANCE—JUNE 1 (Sunday—8:00 AM)

1. Showmanship on Halter (13 + under)
2. Showmanship on Halter (14 − 17)
3. Colts of 1969
4. Colts of 1968

5. Colts of 1967
6. Colts of 1966
7. *Stallions of 1965 and before*
8. *Champion and Reserve Champion*
9. Fillies of 1969
10. Fillies of 1968
11. Fillies of 1967
12. Fillies of 1966
13. *Mare of 1965 and before*
14. *Champion and Reserve Champion*
15. Geldings of 1968
16. Geldings of 1967
17. Geldings of 1966
18. *Geldings of 1965 and before*
19. *Champion and Reserve Champion*
20. Cal-Bred Colts of 1968
21. Cal-Bred Fillies of 1968
22. Race Type Foals of 1968
23. Produce of Dam (Reg. + living) (2 animals—need not be owned by Exh)
24. Get of Sire (Reg. + Living) (3 animals—need not be owned by Exh)

P.O.A. HALTER

25. Showmanship at Hand (P.O.A., 17 + under)
26. P.O.A. Colts and Fillies of 1968
27. P.O.A. Stallions—2 yrs and up
28. P.O.A. Mares—2 yrs and up
29. P.O.A. Geldings—2 yrs and up
30. Junior Western Pleasure (Appaloosa only) (4 years and under)—Horse age
31. Senior Western Pleasure (Appaloosa only) (5 years and over)—Horse age.
32. Nez Perce Stake Race (Appaloosa only)
33. Western Pleasure (Appaloosa only) (Juniors—13 yrs and under)
34. Western Pleasure (Appaloosa only) (Juniors, 14–17 yrs)
35. Bareback Equitation (P.O.A. only)
36. Camas Prairie Stump Race (Appaloosa only)
37. English Pleasure (Appaloosa only)
38. Green Trail Horse—Novice to Ride (Appaloosa only)
39. Trail Horse (Appaloosa only—13 and under)
40. Trail Horse (Appaloosa only, 14–17)
41. Trail Horse (Appaloosa only)

42. Trail Horse (P.O.A. only)
43. Barrel Race—Open (Ladies only—no age limit)
44. Rope Race—(Appaloosa only)
45. Jumpers—Open
46. Jumpers—Appaloosa only
47. Western Pleasure (Gelding Appaloosas)
48. Western Pleasure—(P.O.A. only)
49. Hackamore Class (Appaloosa only) (Horse must be 5 years and under)
50. Dry Stock Horse (Appaloosa only)
51. Costume Class (Appaloosa and P.O.A.)
52. Award of High Point Performance Trophies

PLEASE MAKE CHECKS PAYABLE TO:
    MID VALLEY APPALOOSA SHOW FUND
ALL ENTRIES AND FEES MUST BE SUBMITTED TO:
    DIANA REHN, Secretary
    727 Holly Drive
    Lodi, California 95240
    Phone: (209) 369-4672

A drawing will be held on the second day of the show (June 1). Awarded will be a beautiful saddle or $175.00 cash!—Winner's Choice. Ticket information will be available at the office.

WE'D BE DELIGHTED TO SUPPLY FURTHER INFORMATION UPON REQUEST !!

Refreshments will be available on the grounds—let's get acquainted!

The next example was printed on 8⅝″ by 11⅝″ paper, and was folded twice to make a mailing piece about 4½″ by 5¾″. The entry blank was 8½″ by 11″ and folded right inside.

This was a good-sized affair of two days with 40 classes, yet the format for its prize list was simple and adequate. The sanctioning organization was the Northern California Professional Horsemen's Association, as stated on

SPRING CREEK FARM

24977 PALOMARES RD. - HAYWARD

OPEN HORSE SHOW

REGISTERED JUNIOR POINT SHOW
NORTHERN CALIFORNIA
PROFESSIONAL HORSEMEN'S ASSOCIATION

April 26 — 27 — 1969

JUDGE
MR. LARRY MAYFIELD — FRESNO, CALIF.

AWARDS

Trophy to First - Ribbons thru Fifth

CHAMPIONSHIP AND RESERVE AWARDS IN THE FOLLOWING DIVISIONS
GREEN WORKING HUNTERS (28-29-30)
REGULAR WORKING HUNTERS (31-32-33)
AMATEUR - OWNER WORKING HUNTERS (34-35-36)
JUMPERS (NO POINTS FOR NOVICE) (38-39-40)

Points will be Tabulated on a 5-4-3-2-1 Basis

AWARDS TO HIGH POINT JUNIOR AND HIGH POINT SENIOR RIDER
IN THE WESTERN DIVISION

Make Checks Payable To:
SPRING CREEK FARM
and Mail To:
MRS. GAY PIPER
24977 PALOMARES RD. - HAYWARD, CALIF. 94546
(415) 538-6311

GENERAL RULES

Every Class offered herein which is covered by the Rules of the current A.H.S.A. Rule Book will be conducted and judged in accordance therewith.

Children eligible for Junior Classes shall not have reached their 18th birthday. For Horse Show purposes "Birthday" shall mean the 31st day of December of the year in which the person was born. Birth Date of Junior must be certified on the Entry Blank by parent or guardian.

In Classes 26-27-37 and 38, management reserves the right to require contestants to flip a coin for places other than First in case of a tie.

Protective Head Gear must be worn in all Classes requiring Horses to Jump, and proper attire is required for all Classes.

WESTERN DIVISION
SATURDAY, APRIL 26, 1969 - 8:30 A.M.

Class No. 1	EQUITATION—STOCK SEAT	—	Riders 10 and under.
Class No. 2	EQUITATION—STOCK SEAT	—	Riders 11 - 13.
Class No. 3	EQUITATION—STOCK SEAT	—	Riders 14 - 17.
Class No. 4	PLEASURE HORSES	—	Riders 13 and under.
Class No. 5	PLEASURE HORSES	—	Riders 14 - 17.
Class No. 6	TRAIL HORSES	—	Riders 13 and under.
Class No. 7	TRAIL HORSES	—	Riders 14 - 17.
Class No. 8	STOCK HORSES — Dry Work Only	—	Riders 13 and under.
Class No. 9	STOCK HORSES — Dry Work Only	—	Riders 14 17.

OPEN CLASSES

Class No. 10	PLEASURE HORSES—NOVICE	
Class No. 11	PLEASURE HORSES — $50.00 Added Stake.	
Class No. 12	PLEASURE HORSES — Amateur - Owner $50.00 Added Stake.	
Class No. 13	PLEASURE HORSES — Open to Horses of any Odd Color.	
Class No. 14	PLEASURE HORSES — A.Q.H.A. Registered Quarter Horses.	
Class No. 15	TRAIL HORSES—NOVICE	
Class No. 16	TRAIL HORSES — $50.00 Added Stake.	
Class No. 17	EQUITATION—STOCK SEAT	— Riders 18 and over.
Class No. 18	STOCK HORSES — Dry Work Only	— $50.00 Added Stake.

CLASS SPECIFICATIONS

Western Pleasure Horses will be shown both ways of the Ring at the Walk, Jog and Lope on a reasonably Loose Rein and without undue restraint.

Trail Horses will be shown both ways of the Ring at the Walk, Jog and Lope and over a selected course of obstacles.

In Equitation Classes, the Rider will be judged on Seat, Hands, use of aids and general Horsemanship.

Class No. 13 excludes Blacks, Bays, Browns and Chestnuts.

In Amateur - Owner Class, the Horse must be shown by the owner or a member of his immediate family who is no longer eligible to compete as a Junior Exhibitor.

Novice Classes are open to Horses which have not won three First Ribbons in the appropriate Division.

ENGLISH DIVISION
SUNDAY, APRIL 27, 1969 - 8:30 A.M.

Class No. 19	EQUITATION–HUNTER SEAT	—	Riders 10 and under.
Class No. 20	EQUITATION–HUNTER SEAT	—	Riders 11 - 13.
Class No. 21	EQUITATION–HUNTER SEAT	—	Riders 14 - 17.
Class No. 22	PLEASURE HORSES–HUNTER TYPE	—	Riders 13 and under.
Class No. 23	PLEASURE HORSES–HUNTER TYPE	—	Riders 14 - 17.
Class No. 24	REGULAR WORKING HUNTERS	—	Riders 13 and under - Jumps not to exceed 3' 6".
Class No. 25	REGULAR WORKING HUNTERS	—	Riders 14 - 17 - Jumps appr. 3' 6".
Class No. 26	JUMPERS – Table 1.		Riders 13 and under - Jumps appr. 3' 6".
Class No. 27	JUMPERS – Table 1.		Riders 14 - 17 - Jumps appr. 3' 6".

OPEN CLASSES

Class No. 28	GREEN WORKING HUNTERS UNDER SADDLE	
Class No. 29	GREEN WORKING HUNTERS —	1st year 3' 6" - 2nd year 3' 9" - specify year on Entry Blank.
Class No. 30	GREEN WORKING HUNTERS – $50.00 Added Stake.	
Class No. 31	WORKING HUNTERS UNDER SADDLE	
Class No. 32	REGULAR WORKING HUNTERS — Jumps appr. 3' 9".	
Class No. 33	REGULAR WORKING HUNTERS — $50.00 Added Stake - Jumps appr. 3' 9".	
Class No. 34	WORKING HUNTERS UNDER SADDLE — Amateur - Owner.	
Class No. 35	WORKING HUNTERS – Amateur - Owner - Jumps appr. 3' 6".	
Class No. 36	WORKING HUNTERS — Amateur - Owner - $50.00 Added Stake - Jumps appr. 3' 6".	
Class No. 37	JUMPERS–NOVICE – Jumps appr. 3' 6" - Table 1.	
Class No. 38	JUMPERS – Jumps appr. 3' - 9" - 4' - Table 1.	
Class No. 39	HANDY JUMPERS — Jumps 4' - 4' 3". - Table 2 - Time on 2nd Jump Off.	
Class No. 40	JUMPERS–PUISSANCE — $50.00 Added Stake. Jumps appr. 4' 3" to 4' 6".	

CLASS SPECIFICATIONS

In Hunter Classes, Horses will be judged on Manners, Performance and Way of Going. Conformation will not be considered but Hunting Soundness is required.

Pleasure Horses will be shown both ways of the Ring at the Walk, Trot and Canter and will be judged on Performance, Manners, Quality and Soundness.

In Under Saddle Classes, no more than 8 Horses will be asked to Hand Gallop at one time. (Green Horses are not required to Hand Gallop).

A Green Hunter is a Horse who has not shown over Fences prior to January 1, 1968. Specify 1st or 2nd year on Entry Blank.

In Amateur - Owner Class, the Horse must be shown by the owner or a member of his immediate family who is no longer eligible to compete as a Junior Exhibitor.

In Equitation Classes the Rider will be judged on Seat, Hands use of aids and general Horsemanship.

ENTRY FEES

Classes 11 - 12 - 16 - 18 - 30 - 33 - 36 - 40 — $10.00
All Others $4.00
Post Entry Penalties — Trophy and Ribbon Classes $1.00 — Stake Classes $2.00
In Stake Classes — $6.00 will be added back and divided 30 - 25 - 20 - 15 - 10.

ENTRIES CLOSE APRIL 22, 1969

the front page, and it did not have any special requirements for the prize list other than this statement.

Here is a copy of a schooling show prize list. This was
a single mimeographed sheet—8½" by 14"—or legal size,
with nothing on the back. This was folded twice so that
the mailing piece was 3½" by 8", stapled so it would not
come unfolded in transit.

Note that this had no sanctioning organization for any
point awards other than the club itself. Also note that
no rules were mentioned under which the affair was to
be held. In this case, it was assumed that from the nature of the events, the rules of the American Horse
Shows Association would govern as to the required performances and judging.

In this instance the entry blank is on the same sheet
as the list of classes, and not a separate sheet. Although
there is room for only three class entries, additional
classes may be added on another sheet or on the back.

ENGLISH DIVISION

CLASS No. 1	KINDERGARTEN JUMPERS	Jumps 2' - 2'6". Table 1. Horse and/or Rider not to have won any ribbon over fences prior to Jan. 1, 1970.
CLASS No. 2	MAIDEN JUMPERS	Jumps 3' - 3'3". Table 1. Horse and/or Rider not to have won a blue ribbon over fences prior to Jan. 1, 1970.
CLASS No. 3	NOVICE JUMPERS	Jumps 3'3" - 3'6". Table 1. Horse not to have won 3 blue ribbons in the Jumper Division prior to Jan. 1, 1970.
CLASS No. 4	$25.00 ADDED JUMPER STAKE	Jumps 3'6" - 4'. Table 1. Open.
CLASS No. 5	WORKING HUNTERS–MAIDEN	Jumps 2'6" - 3'. Horse and/or Rider not to have won a blue ribbon in the Hunter Division prior to Jan. 1, 1970.
CLASS No. 6	WORKING HUNTERS	Jumps 3'3" - 3'6". Open.
CLASS No. 7	EQUITATION–HUNTER SEAT–MAIDEN	Riders 17 and under. Rider not to have won a blue ribbon in any Equitation Division prior to Jan. 1. 1970.
CLASS No. 8	EQUITATION–HUNTER SEAT	Riders 17 and under.
CLASS No. 9	ENGLISH PLEASURE–NOVICE	Horse not to have won 3 blue ribbons in the Pleasure Horse Division prior to Jan. 1, 1970.
CLASS No. 10	HUNTER HACKS	2 Fences approximately 2'6". Open.
CLASS No. 11	ENGLISH PLEASURE HORSES	Open.

WESTERN DIVISION

CLASS No. 12	SHOWMANSHIP IN HALTER	Exhibitor 17 and under judged on condition and grooming 40%, showmanship 60%.
CLASS No. 13	TRAIL HORSES–NOVICE	Horse not to have won 3 blue ribbons in the Trail Horse Division prior to Jan. 1, 1970.
CLASS No. 14	TRAIL HORSES	Open.
CLASS No. 15	EQUITATION–STOCK SEAT–MAIDEN	Riders 17 and under. Rider not to have won a blue ribbon in any Equitation Division prior to Jan. 1, 1970. (Show Chaps, Etc. not required in this class).
CLASS No. 16	EQUITATION–STOCK SEAT–NOVICE	Riders 17 and under. Rider not to have won 3 blue ribbons in the Equitation Division prior to Jan. 1, 1970.
CLASS No. 17	EQUITATION–STOCK SEAT	Riders 17 and under.
CLASS No. 18	WESTERN PLEASURE–KINDERGARTEN	Horse and/or Rider not to have won a ribbon in the Pleasure Horse Division prior to Jan. 1, 1970. (Show Chaps, etc. not required in this class).
CLASS No. 19	WESTERN PLEASURE–NOVICE	Horse not to have won 3 blue ribbons in the Pleasure Horse Division prior to Jan. 1, 1970.
CLASS No. 20	WESTERN PLEASURE–MAIDEN	Horse and/or Rider not to have won a blue ribbon in the Pleasure Horse Division prior to Jan. 1, 1970.
CLASS No. 21	$25.00 ADDED NOVICE WESTERN PLEASURE STAKE	Horse not to have won 3 blue ribbons in the Pleasure Horse Division prior to Jan. 1, 1970.
CLASS No. 22	$25.00 ADDED WESTERN PLEASURE STAKE	Open.

In Classes 1 - 2 - 5 - 18 - 20, the Horse or the Rider may qualify. If the Rider qualifies, he may ride any Horse. If the Horse qualifies, any Rider may ride him.

In Classes 4 - 21 - 22, $4.00 of Entry Fee will be added back and divided 30-25-20-15-10.

Trophy and Ribbon to First — Ribbon and Equipment award Second thru Fifth.
(A usable piece of Barn Equipment will be awarded with all Second thru Fifth place Ribbons).

Points to count toward High Point English or High Point Western Award of combined shows on Jan. 25 - Feb. 22 and March 22, 1970, and Kimberwicke Stables English and Western Perpetual Trophies (yearly Award).

ENTRY BLANK

ENTRY FEES
Trophy and Ribbon Classes	$3.00
Stake Classes	$7.00
Post Entry Penalty	.50 per class
Entries Close — Jan. 21, 1970	

MAIL ENTRIES TO: KIMBERWICKE STABLES – 1920 GREEN VALLEY RD., DANVILLE CA. 94526
For Information Call: (415) 531-2119 or (415) 837-9146

CLASS No.	HORSE	RIDER	OWNER	FEE
			TOTAL	

Kimberwicke Stables will not be responsible for any loss or damage or injury to horses exhibited or for any article of any kind or nature that may be destroyed or lost or in any way injured. Each exhibitor will be responsible for any injury that may be occasioned to any person whomsoever, by any horse owned or exhibited by him and shall indemnify the management against all claims and demands of any kind or nature occasioned by any horse owned or exhibited by him, or arise from negligence of the person in charge of such horse. All horses exhibited in this show will be entirely at the owner's risk.

SIGNATURE OF
OWNER_____ PARENT OR GUARDIAN_____

OWNER OR AGENT_____ AGE OF JUNIOR EXHIBITOR_____

ADDRESS_____ CITY_____ ZIP_____ PHONE_____

The next example is similar, with the entry form at the bottom of the page. This one was printed by offset so more could be put on the page.

CONCORD-MT. DIABLO TRAIL RIDE ASSOCIATION WINTER SCHOOLING SHOW

Sunday, Feb. 9, 1964—Rain Date—Feb. 16, 1964
Trail Ride Grounds—Mt. Diablo—9:00 A.M.

Classes will be run simultaneously as noted.

Judges: Evelyn Leydecker—English
Jack Manners—Western

Class No.

1 Jr. Jumpers—17 and under

3 Western Equitation—13 yrs and under
5 Model Stock Horses
7 Western Pleasure Horses, Open
9 Western Equitation—14 thru 17 years
11 Knockdown and Out—Begin at 3'6"
13 Jr. Working Hunters—17 and under
15 Handy Working Hunters—3'6"

17 Open Jumpers—3'6"

19 Jr. Western Pleasure Horses 13 years and under
21 Open Working Hunters—3'6"

23 Handy Jumpers—3'6"

Class No.

2 Bareback Equitation—No age limit
4 English Equitation—14 thru 17 years
6 Working Hunter Hacks
8 English Pleasure Horses, Open
10 English Equitation—13 yrs and under
12 Western Pleasure, Novice (Hackamore permitted)
14 Western Equitation, Open, Novice
16 Potluck Pairs—Post entries accepted
18 Trail Horses, Novice—Hackamore permitted
20*CMDTRA English or Western Pleasure Horses
22 Jr. English Pleasure Horses 14 thru 17 years
24 Trail Horses, Open
25 Jr. Western Pleasure—14 thru 17 years
26 Jr. English Pleasure—13 yrs and under

* Open only to horses owned and shown by members of the Concord-

Mt. Diablo Trail Ride Association. Perpetual Club Trophy to winner. Must win twice to retain.

Sandy soil in both rings permits use in most all weather. Reasonable attempts will be made to notify if cancellation is necessary. If in doubt, call MU 5-6114, MU 5-6716 or YE 5-3288.

Entry Fee $2.50 per class. *No Post Entries*—Entries close midnight, Feb. 3, 1964. *All contestants will be guests for lunch.* Available to others at 75¢ per plate.

As'gnd No.	Class No.	Name of Horse	Rider	Owner	Entry Fee

Rules: The Concord-Mt. Diablo Trail Ride Association shall not be responsible for any accident that may occur to or be caused by any horse exhibited at the Show, and the exhibitor shall hold the Concord-Mt. Diablo Trail Ride Association harmless, and indemnify it against any legal action arising from such accident. Although doing all in its power to protect exhibitors, the Concord-Mt. Diablo Trail Ride Association shall not be held responsible for any loss or damage to any vehicle or article belonging to an exhibitor, or employee.

_____

Exhibitor's Name

_____

Address

_____

City & State

_____

Phone

Signature of Exhibitor

I hereby consent to the entry of my child in the Concord-Mt. Diablo Trail Ride Assoc. Show.

_____

Signature of Parent or Guardian of Minor

No entries accepted unless this form is signed. Entry fees must accompany entry.

MAIL ENTRIES TO: Mrs. Elmer Becker, Box 235, Clayton, Calif.
Phone: MU 5-6114
FUTURE SCHOOLING SHOW—March 15, 1964

The next example is that of a prize list for a one-day show, sanctioned by both the American Horse Shows Association and the Pacific Coast Hunter, Jumper and Stock Horse Association, covering 46 classes. It is quite an ingenious method of getting all the required information into a small space.

The final result was an eight-page booklet—4″ by 9″—that was easily mailed with the entry form in a standard envelope. It is included among the various examples to show what can be done with a little resourcefulness and inventiveness.

POTOMAC WEST
SCHOOL OF HORSEMANSHIP

presents

The First Annual
SPRING JUNIOR HORSE SHOW

May 17, 1969

Regular Show Member
AMERICAN HORSE SHOWS
ASSOCIATION, INC.

P.C.H.J.S.H.A. "B" JR.

NORTHERN CALIFORNIA PROFESSIONAL
HORSEMAN'S ASSOCIATION (JUNIOR)

"EVERY CLASS OFFERED HEREIN WHICH
IS COVERED BY THE RULES AND SPECI-
FICATIONS OF THE CURRENT A.H.S.A.
RULE BOOK WILL BE CONDUCTED IN AC-
CORDANCE THEREWITH"

TROPHY TO FIRST

RIBBONS TO SEVENTH
ENTRIES CLOSE MAY 10, 1969

JUDGES AND OFFICIALS

THE HORSE SHOW MANAGEMENT RESERVES THE RIGHT TO CANCEL ANY
CLASS WITH LESS THAN FIVE ENTRIES.

THE FOLLOWING HAVE ACCEPTED OUR INVITATION TO OFFICIATE IN THE
FIRST ANNUAL POTOMAC WEST SPRING JUNIOR HORSE SHOW. THE MAN-
AGEMENT RESERVES THE RIGHT TO VARY OR ADD TO THESE NAMES IF IT
DEEMS ADVISABLE FOR THE GOOD OF THE SHOW.

Judges

Mr. Ronnie Richards	WESTERN, STOCK SEAT EQUITATION
Mrs. J. J. Kessler	HUNTERS, HUNTER SEAT EQUITATION
Mrs. Judy Kennedy	WESTERN, HUNTERS, JUMPERS

Officials

Show Manager .... FORREST LONG
Show Secretary .... BETTE LONG
AHSA Steward .... G. E. PENDERGAST
Trophies .... SALLY KENEFICK
Photographer .... JUNE FALLAW

Schedule of Charges

Championship Classes $5.00
All other classes $4.00
Post Entry Penalty (per class) $1.00

ENTRIES CLOSE MAY 10, 1969
NO REFUNDS AFTER CLOSING DATE.

THE POTOMAC WEST JUNIOR HORSE SHOW
IS OPERATED IN ACCORDANCE WITH THE CURRENT RULES OF
THE AMERICAN HORSE SHOWS ASSOCIATION
OF WHICH BODY IT IS A
REGULAR SHOW MEMBER   RATED AS A "C" SHOW

EVERY PERSON WHO PARTICIPATES IN THE SHOW IS RESPONSIBLE FOR A
KNOWLEDGE OF AND IS SUBJECT TO THE ASSOCIATION RULES. SPECTATORS
WILL BETTER ENJOY THE SHOW BY KNOWING THEM. MEMBERS RECEIVE A
COPY OF THE CURRENT RULE BOOK AND "HORSE SHOW" AND ARE ENTITLED
TO PARTICIPATE IN THE ANNUAL HORSE OF THE YEAR COMPETITIONS.
NO POINTS WILL BE COUNTED TOWARD THE ANNUAL HORSE OF THE YEAR
AWARD COMPETITIONS BEFORE MEMBERSHIP DUES HAVE BEEN PAID AND
HORSES RECORDED WITH THE AHSA.

ANNUAL CONVENTION
THE WALDORF ASTORIA
NEW YORK, NEW YORK
JANUARY 15-17, 1970

* * * * * * * *

AMERICAN HORSE SHOWS ASSOCIATION, INC.

527 MADISON AVE., NEW YORK, N.Y.   TEL. 212 PLAZA 9-3070

ALBERT E. HART, JR., PRES.   WALTER B. DEVEREUX, SECTY.

I HEREBY APPLY FOR.............................MEMBERSHIP AND ENCLOSE PAYMENT FOR $.................... (MEMBERSHIP EXPIRES DECEMBER 31)

LIFE	$250	SENIOR	$15.00
CONTRIBUTING	$ 25	JUNIOR—UNDER 18 YRS.	$ 7.50

JUNIORS GIVE DATE AND YEAR OF BIRTH .... 19........

(DUES INCLUDE $1 FOR SUBSCRIPTION TO "HORSE SHOW")

NAME ....

(PRINT)

ADDRESS ....

STREET   ROUTE   BOX NO.

CITY, STATE, ZIP CODE ....

* * * * * * * *

PACIFIC COAST HUNTER, JUMPER AND
STOCK HORSE ASSOCIATION, INC.

3301 SHELDON STREET, SACRAMENTO, CALIFORNIA 95838

NAME ....

ADDRESS ....

CITY.. PHONE...............................

SENIOR MEMBERSHIP ANNUAL DUES—

FAMILY MEMBERSHIP—1ST MEMBERSHIP $15.00

AFTER THAT—

EACH ADDITIONAL MEMBER OF FAMILY—

JUNIOR MEMBERSHIP ANNUAL DUES $10.00

UNDER 18 YEARS, NO VOTING PRIVILEGES .... $ 7.50

SIGNED ....

CLASS SCHEDULE
Morning 8:00 A.M.
RING "A"

CLASS NO.

1-A NOVICE WESTERN PLEASURE—13 & UNDER

2-A NOVICE WESTERN PLEASURE—14 THRU 17

3-A NOVICE STOCK SEAT EQUITATION—13 & UNDER

4-A NOVICE STOCK SEAT EQUITATION—14 THRU 17
5-A NOVICE HUNTER SEAT EQUITATION—13 & UNDER
6-A HUNTER SEAT EQUITATION—11 THRU 13
7-A HUNTER SEAT EQUITATION—10 & UNDER
8-A NOVICE HUNTER SEAT EQUITATION—14 THRU 17
9-A HUNTER SEAT EQUITATION—14 THRU 17

RING "B"

1-B NOVICE ENGLISH PLEASURE (HUNTER TYPE) 13 & UNDER
2-B ENGLISH PLEASURE (HUNTER TYPE) 11 THRU 13
3-B ENGLISH PLEASURE (HUNTER TYPE) 10 & UNDER
4-B NOVICE ENGLISH PLEASURE (HUNTER TYPE) 14 THRU 17
5-B ENGLISH PLEASURE (HUNTER TYPE) 14 THRU 17
6-B STOCK SEAT EQUITATION—10 & UNDER
7-B WESTERN PLEASURE—11 THRU 13
8-B WESTERN PLEASURE—14 THRU 17
9-B WESTERN PLEASURE—10 & UNDER
10-B STOCK SEAT EQUITATION—11 THRU 13
11-B STOCK SEAT EQUITATION—14 THRU 17

RING "C"

1-C JR. WORKING HUNTERS—14 THRU 17
2-C JR. WORKING HUNTERS—13 & UNDER
3-C JR. JUMPERS—14 THRU 17 (TABLE 1)
4-C JR. JUMPERS—13 & UNDER (TABLE 1)
5-C BARBARA WORTH GOOD HANDS AND SEAT

Afternoon 1:00 P.M.
RING "A"

10-A WESTERN PLEASURE CHAMPIONSHIP
11-A RONNIE RICHARDS, JR. STOCK SEAT MEDAL
12-A STOCK HORSE—14 THRU 17
13-A STOCK HORSE—13 & UNDER
14-A HUNTER SEAT EQUITATION CHAMPIONSHIP
15-A WORKING HUNTER HACKS—17 & UNDER
16-A A.H.S.A. STOCK SEAT MEDAL
17-A STOCK HORSE CHAMPIONSHIP

RING "B"

12-B ENGLISH PLEASURE (HUNTER TYPE) CHAMPIONSHIP
13-B TRAIL HORSES—14 THRU 17
14-B TRAIL HORSES—13 & UNDER

15-B STOCK SEAT EQUITATION CHAMPIONSHIP
16-B TRAIL HORSE CHAMPIONSHIP

RING "C"

6-C A.H.S.A. HUNTER SEAT MEDAL
7-C CROSS COUNTRY HUNTERS—17 & UNDER
8-C ONONDARKA MEDAL
9-C JR. JUMPERS (SIX BAR) 14 THRU 17
10-C JR. JUMPERS (SIX BAR) 13 & UNDER
11-C POTOMAC WEST HORSEMANSHIP
12-C JR. WORKING HUNTER CHAMPIONSHIP
13-C JR. JUMPER CHAMPIONSHIP

CLASS SPECIFICATIONS
Western Division

WESTERN PLEASURE HORSE

OPEN TO HORSES AND PONIES. TO BE SHOWN AT A WALK, JOG TROT AND
LOPE BOTH WAYS OF THE RING ON A REASONABLE LOOSE REIN WITHOUT
UNDUE RESTRAINT. TO BE JUDGED ON PERFORMANCE 60%, CONFORMA-
TION 30% AND APPOINTMENTS 10%

RIDERS 10 YEARS AND UNDER .... CLASS   9-B
RIDERS 11 THROUGH 13 YEARS .... CLASS   7-B
RIDERS 14 THROUGH 17 YEARS .... CLASS   8-B
*CHAMPIONSHIP .... CLASS 10-A
**NOVICE—RIDERS 13 YEARS AND UNDER .... CLASS   1-A
**NOVICE—RIDERS 14 THROUGH 17 YEARS .... CLASS   2-A
*TO BE ELIGIBLE TO ENTER CHAMPIONSHIP CLASS 10-A HORSE MUST HAVE
BEEN ENTERED, SHOWN AND JUDGED IN CLASS 9-B, 7-B, OR 8-B.
**NOVICE CLASSES OPEN TO HORSES WHICH HAVE NOT WON THREE FIRST
RIBBONS IN THIS CLASSIFICATION AT RECOGNIZED SHOWS.

STOCK SEAT EQUITATION

RIDERS TO SHOW HORSES OR PONIES AT A WALK, JOG TROT AND LOPE
BOTH WAYS OF THE RING. TO BE JUDGED ON GENERAL HORSEMANSHIP
ONLY.

RIDERS 10 YEARS AND UNDER .... CLASS   6-B
RIDERS 11 THROUGH 13 YEARS .... CLASS 10-B
RIDERS 14 THROUGH 17 YEARS .... CLASS 11-B
*CHAMPIONSHIP .... CLASS 15-B
**NOVICE—RIDERS 13 YEARS AND UNDER .... CLASS   3-A
**NOVICE—RIDERS 14 THROUGH 17 YEARS .... CLASS   4-A

*TO BE ELIGIBLE TO ENTER CHAMPIONSHIP CLASS 15-B RIDER MUST
HAVE BEEN ENTERED, SHOWN AND JUDGED IN CLASS 6-B, 10-B, OR 11-B.
**NOVICE CLASSES OPEN TO RIDERS WHO HAVE NOT WON THREE FIRST
RIBBONS IN THIS CLASSIFICATION AT RECOGNIZED SHOWS.

TRAIL HORSES

OPEN TO HORSES OR PONIES. TO BE SHOWN AT A WALK, JOG TROT AND
LOPE BOTH WAYS OF THE RING ON A REASONABLY LOOSE REIN, WITHOUT
UNDUE RESTRAINT. TO BE SHOWN OVER AND THROUGH OBSTACLES. TO
BE JUDGED ON PERFORMANCE, WITH EMPHASIS ON MANNERS 60%;
APPOINTMENTS, EQUIPMENT NEATNESS (SILVER NOT TO COUNT) 20%
AND CONFORMATION 20%

RIDERS 13 YEARS AND UNDER .... CLASS 14-B
RIDERS 14 THROUGH 17 YEARS .... CLASS 13-B
*CHAMPIONSHIP .... CLASS 16-B
*TO BE ELIGIBLE TO ENTER CHAMPIONSHIP CLASS 16-B HORSE MUST
HAVE BEEN ENTERED, SHOWN AND JUDGED IN CLASS 13-B, OR 14-B.

STOCK HORSES

OPEN TO HORSES OR PONIES. TO BE SHOWN AT A WALK, JOG TROT AND
LOPE WITHOUT RESTRAINT; LOPE A FIGURE EIGHT; RUN AT SPEED, STOP
AND TURN EASILY. TO BE JUDGED ON MANNERS WITH PARTICULAR EM-
PHASIS ON RIDER'S HANDS, REIN, CONFORMATION AND APPOINTMENTS.

RIDERS 13 YEARS AND UNDER .... CLASS 13-A
RIDERS 14 THROUGH 17 YEARS .... CLASS 12-A
*CHAMPIONSHIP .... CLASS 17-A
*TO BE ELIGIBLE TO ENTER CHAMPIONSHIP CLASS 17-A HORSE MUST
HAVE BEEN ENTERED, SHOWN AND JUDGED IN CLASS 13-A, OR 12-A.

MEDAL CLASSES

RONNIE RICHARDS, JR. STOCK SEAT MEDAL .... CLASS 11-A
OPEN TO RIDERS 12 YEARS AND UNDER WHO ARE JUNIOR MEMBERS OF
THE PACIFIC COAST HUNTER, JUMPER AND STOCK HORSE ASSOCIATION.
TO BE JUDGED THE SAME AS THE AHSA STOCK SEAT MEDAL CLASS,
WITH THE EXCEPTION OF MOUNTING AND DISMOUNTING.
A.H.S.A. STOCK SEAT MEDAL .... CLASS 16-A
OPEN TO JUNIOR MEMBERS OF THE AMERICAN HORSE SHOWS ASSOCIA-
TION WHO HAVE NOT YET REACHED THEIR 18TH BIRTHDAY. APPLICATION
FOR MEMBERSHIP MUST BE MADE DIRECT TO THE AHSA. IN CALIFORNIA
A RIDER MUST WIN TWO BLUES AND IN ALL OTHER STATES AND CANADA
ONE BLUE TO QUALIFY FOR THE FINAL RIDE-OFF AT A SPECIFIED SHOW
AT THE END OF THE SEASON. ON QUALIFYING A RIDER WILL RECEIVE A

SILVER MEDAL; AN ENGROSSED CERTIFICATE WILL BE PRESENTED FOR PRELIMINARY WINS. ALL CONTESTANTS ARE REQUIRED TO PERFORM THE ENTIRE PATTERN; OTHER INDIVIDUAL TESTS ARE OPTIONAL. TESTS 1–12. TO FILL A CLASS FIVE COMPETITORS MUST SHOW IN PROPER TACK.

English Division
ENGLISH PLEASURE (HUNTER TYPE)

HORSES TO BE SHOWN AT A WALK, TROT AND CANTER BOTH WAYS OF THE RING. TO BE JUDGED ON MANNERS, QUALITY, PERFORMANCE AND SUITABILITY TO RIDER. LOOSE REIN ON COMMAND.

RIDERS 10 YEARS AND UNDER .... CLASS   3-B
RIDERS 11 THROUGH 13 YEARS .... CLASS   2-B
RIDERS 14 THROUGH 17 YEARS .... CLASS   5-B
*CHAMPIONSHIP .... CLASS 12-B
**NOVICE—RIDERS 13 YEARS AND UNDER .... CLASS   1-B
**NOVICE—RIDERS 14 THROUGH 17 YEARS .... CLASS   4-B

*TO BE ELIGIBLE TO ENTER CHAMPIONSHIP CLASS 12-B HORSE MUST HAVE BEEN ENTERED, SHOWN AND JUDGED IN CLASS 2-B, 3-B, OF 5-B.
**NOVICE CLASSES OPEN TO HORSES WHICH HAVE NOT WON THREE FIRST RIBBONS IN THIS CLASSIFICATION AT RECOGNIZED SHOWS.

HUNTER SEAT EQUITATION

RIDERS TO SHOW HORSES AT A WALK, TROT AND CANTER BOTH WAYS OF THE RING. TO BE JUDGED ON GENERAL HORSEMANSHIP ONLY.

RIDERS 10 YEARS AND UNDER .... CLASS   7-A
RIDERS 11 THROUGH 13 YEARS .... CLASS   6-A
RIDERS 14 THROUGH 17 YEARS .... CLASS   9-A
*CHAMPIONSHIP .... CLASS 14-A
**NOVICE—RIDERS 13 YEARS AND UNDER .... CLASS   5-A
**NOVICE—RIDERS 14 THROUGH 17 YEARS .... CLASS   8-A

*TO BE ELIGIBLE TO ENTER CHAMPIONSHIP CLASS 14-A RIDER MUST HAVE BEEN ENTERED, SHOWN AND JUDGED IN CLASS 6-A, 7-A, OR 9-A.
**NOVICE CLASSES ARE OPEN TO RIDERS WHO HAVE NOT WON THREE FIRST RIBBONS IN THIS CLASSIFICATION AT RECOGNIZED SHOWS.

JUNIOR WORKING HUNTERS

TO BE JUDGED ON AN EVEN HUNTING PACE, MANNERS, WAY OF GOING AND STYLE OF JUMPING OVER A MINIMUM OF EIGHT FENCES. EXTREME SPEED SHALL BE PENALIZED. CONFORMATION NOT TO BE CONSIDERED, BUT HUNTING SOUNDNESS IS REQUIRED.

RIDERS 13 YEARS AND UNDER (FENCES 3'6") .... CLASS   2-C
RIDERS 14 THROUGH 17 YEARS (FENCES 3'9") .... CLASS   1-C

RIDERS 17 YEARS AND UNDER .... CLASS 7-C
(CROSS COUNTRY—FENCES 3'0"–3'9")

*CHAMPIONSHIP .... CLASS 12-C
*TO BE ELIGIBLE HORSE MUST HAVE BEEN ENTERED, SHOWN AND JUDGED
IN CLASS 1-C, 2-C, OR 7-C.

WORKING HUNTER HACKS—RIDERS 17 YEARS AND UNDER. TO BE SHOWN
AT A WALK, TROT AND CANTER BOTH WAYS OF THE RING. AT LEAST
EIGHT HORSES, IF AVAILABLE, ARE REQUIRED TO JUMP TWO FENCES
3'6" AND GALLOP ONE WAY OF THE RING. .... CLASS 15-A

JUNIOR JUMPERS

TO BE SHOWN OVER A MINIMUM OF EIGHT JUMPS. IN THE EVENT OF
EQUALITY OF FAULTS, SUCCESSIVE JUMP-OFFS WILL BE HELD. TABLE 1.
TOUCHES TO COUNT.

RIDERS 13 YEARS AND UNDER .... CLASS 4-C
(FENCES 3'6"–3'9"; SPREADS 4')

RIDERS 14 THROUGH 17 YEARS .... CLASS 3-C
(FENCES 3'9"–4'0"; SPREADS 4')

JUNIOR JUMPERS, SIX BARS

TO BE SHOWN OVER 6 IDENTICAL VERTICAL JUMPS. IN THE EVENT OF
TIES COMPULSORY SUCCESSIVE JUMP-OFFS ARE CONDUCTED OVER THE
ORIGINAL COURSE WITH JUMPS RAISED. TABLE 11, SEC. 7. TOUCHES
NOT TO COUNT.

RIDERS 13 YEARS AND UNDER .... CLASS 10-C
(JUMPS 3'0" TO 3'6")

RIDERS 14 THROUGH 17 YEARS .... CLASS 9-C
(JUMPS 3'3" TO 3'9")

JUNIOR JUMPER CHAMPIONSHIP .... CLASS 13-C
(JUMPS 3'6"–4'0"; SPREADS 4'—TABLE I)

TO BE ELIGIBLE TO ENTER JR. JUMPER CHAMPIONSHIP CLASS, HORSE MUST
HAVE BEEN ENTERED, SHOWN AND JUDGED IN CLASS 3C, 4C, 9C, OR 10C.

BARBARA WORTH GOOD HANDS AND SEAT MEDAL .... CLASS 5-C
FOR RIDERS 17 YEARS OF AGE AND UNDER WHO ARE MEMBERS OF THE
P.C.H.J. & S.H.A. TO BE JUDGED OVER A COURSE OF EIGHT JUMPS. WINNER
WILL RECEIVE B.W.G.H. & S. MEDALLION AND IS AUTOMATICALLY INELIGI-
BLE TO SHOW IN ANY OTHER B.W.G.H. & S. CLASSES DURING THE YEAR. ALL
WINNERS FOR THE YEAR ARE ELIGIBLE TO COMPETE IN THE FINALS.
WINNER OF THE FINALS IS INELIGIBLE TO SHOW IN FUTURE B.W.G.H. & S.
CLASSES.

AHSA HUNTER SEAT MEDAL CLASS .... CLASS 6-C
OPEN TO JUNIOR MEMBERS OF THE AMERICAN HORSE SHOWS ASSOCIATION
WHO HAVE NOT YET REACHED THEIR 18TH BIRTHDAY. APPLICATION FOR
MEMBERSHIP MUST BE MADE DIRECT TO THE AHSA. TO BE SHOWN OVER A
FIGURE EIGHT COURSE OF NOT LESS THAN 6 OBSTACLES AT 3′6″ WHICH
MUST INCLUDE ONE COMBINATION AND TWO CHANGES OF DIRECTION. IN
CONN., N.J., N.Y., AND PA. A RIDER MUST WIN THREE BLUES, IN CALIF.
TWO BLUES, AND IN ALL OTHER STATES AND CANADA ONE BLUE TO QUAL-
IFY FOR THE FINAL RIDE-OFF AT A SPECIFIED SHOW AT THE END OF THE
SEASON. ON QUALIFYING A RIDER WILL RECEIVE A SILVER MEDAL; AN EN-
GROSSED CERTIFICATE WILL BE PRESENTED FOR PRELIMINARY WINS. TWO
OR MORE TESTS OF THE TOP FOUR CONTESTANTS ARE REQUIRED. TESTS
1-15. ONLY ONE RIDER PER HORSE. TO FILL A CLASS FIVE COMPETITORS
MUST COMPLETE THE COURSE.

ONONDARKA MEDAL CLASS .... CLASS 8-C
OPEN TO RIDERS 12 YEARS OF AGE AND UNDER WHO BELONG TO THE
P.C.H.J. & S.H.A. TO BE JUDGED OVER A FIGURE EIGHT COURSE OF 3′
FENCES. TWO OR MORE TESTS OF THE TOP FOUR CONTESTANTS REQUIRED.
TESTS 1-15. ONLY ONE RIDER PER HORSE. TO FILL A CLASS, FIVE COM-
PETITORS MUST COMPLETE THE COURSE. WINNER WILL RECEIVE GOLD
MEDAL AND BE ELIGIBLE TO COMPETE IN THE FINALS.

POTOMAC WEST HORSEMANSHIP .... CLASS 11-C
OPEN TO RIDERS WHO HAVE NOT REACHED THEIR 18TH BIRTHDAY. TO BE
JUDGED ON GENERAL HORSEMANSHIP CONSISTING OF A PRESCRIBED EQUI-
TATION ROUTINE AND JUMPING A COURSE OF A MINIMUM OF EIGHT
JUMPS. FENCES 3′6″.

APPENDIX B
ENTRY FORMS

On the following pages are examples of entry forms.
The first one is that for the 1969 California State Fair
Horse Show. This form is furnished to the exhibitor in
duplicate with a carbon sheet in between. It is quite
comprehensive and is set up not only for a show secretary's use but also for easy auditing, a necessity in an
affair of this kind.

Form F-25
(Rev. 6-67)

PRINT OR TYPEWRITE YOUR ENTRIES
(Except for Signatures)

HORSE SHOW
(One Owner Only)

ENTRY FORM
On Each Form)

116th CALIFORNIA STATE FAIR HORSE SHOW

52nd DISTRICT AGRICULTURAL ASSOCIATION
P. O. BOX 4834
Sacramento, California 95825
Phone (916) 641-2415

MAKE ALL CHECKS PAYABLE TO
52nd DISTRICT AGRICULTURAL ASSOCIATION

"I hereby certify that every horse, rider and/or driver is eligible as entered and agree for myself and my representatives to be bound by the Constitution and Rules of The American Horse Shows Association and this Show."

Please accept the entries described below subject to the rules and regulations as published in the official premium list for your fair.

PRINTED NAME OF REGISTERED AND/OR LEGAL OWNER

WRITTEN SIGNATURE OF OWNER OR AGENT

OWNER'S STREET OR R.F.D. NUMBER

OWNER'S CITY OR POST OFFICE

ZIP CODE

FOR HORSE SHOW
ENTRIES ONLY

DATE OF ENTRY

SIGNATURE _____ of owner or Agent

TELEPHONE NO.

Registration Number	NAME OF HORSE	NAME OF RIDER	Description of Animal						(In Premium List)			Leave These Spaces Blank		
			Height	Weight	Color	Sex	Age	Class No.	Section No.	Entry Fee	Entry No.	Place	Award
1													
2													
3													
4													
5													
6													
7													
8													
9													
10													
11													
12													
13													

14. Horses Showing in Welsh Pony, P.O.A., Appaloosa, Morgan, Pinto, Quarter, Shetland, Paint, & Arabian Classes Must Show Registration Number.

15. NOTE: Green Hunters 1st Year ( ) 2nd Year ( ). All Entries for Breeding Class MUST be Entered on Yellow Livestock Form.

CONSULT PREMIUM BOOK FOR CLASS OR SECTION NUMBERS, ENTRY FEES, STALL RENTAL RATES, AND ENTRY CLOSING DATES

Number of Animals _____ (_____)

Entry Fees _____
Box Stalls Required $15.00 _____
Tie Stalls Required $12.00 _____ Pony _____
Tail Boards Required $ 2.50 _____
OTHER CHARGES (Service Charge $5 per Horse) _____

Total Awards _____

Payment, Check No. _____

Amount Enclosed _____

Receipt No. _____

Please Stable My Horse with
Name _____
Stalls will be bedded with straw ONLY
Exhibitors Must Purchase Shavings

EXHIBITOR'S NO. _____

CHECKS FOR ENTRY AND STALL FEES AND OTHER FEES MUST ACCOMPANY THIS ENTRY FORM

California State Horsemen's Association
CHAMPIONSHIP HORSE SHOW

AUGUST 19 – 24, 1968

ENTRIES CLOSE JULY 22, 1968

Sonoma County Fairgrounds - Santa Rosa, Calif.

Enter Horse's Name and list all classes in which it is entered before entering the next horse

NAME OF HORSE	NAME OF RIDER	DESCRIPTION OF ANIMAL					(IN PRIZE LIST)	
		HEIGHT	WEIGHT	COLOR	SEX	AGE	CLASS NO.	ENTRY FEE

ALL MEMBERS OF TEAM EVENTS MUST BE ENTERED ON THE SAME ENTRY BLANK.

ENTRY FEES TOTAL

I hereby make the above entries and in consideration of the acceptance of these entries, I hereby release and agree to hold free and harmless, the California State Horsemen's Association and the Sonoma County Fair from any liability occasioned, or expense resulting from or occasioned, by injury or death of myself or other persons; or damage to my property or property owned by other persons, resulting from such entry, participation or use of property.

I hereby certify that every horse, rider and/or driver is eligible as entered and agree for myself and my representative to be bound by the Constitution and Rules of the American Horse Shows Association and this show.

The undersigned hereby states that he has read and has full understanding of the rules and regulations governing this show; that he agrees to be governed by said rules and regulations; and he further states that the information given in connection with the entries herein presented, is a statement of fact to his personal knowledge.

ARRIVAL DATE ....

DEPARTURE DATE...

Total of Entry Fees...................................$.................

Box Stalls Required......(...........@ $12.50) $.............

Tail Boards...................(...........@ $2.50) $.............

Vacation Trailer Space (...........@ $5.00) $.............

TOTAL ENCLOSED $.................

P.C.H.J. No.................A.H.S.A. No.................AMATEUR No.............

NAME TO APPEAR ON PROGRAM (Owner)..................................

(PLEASE PRINT)

SIGNATURE OF OWNER OR AGENT...

SIGNATURE OF PARENT OR GUARDIAN OF MINOR.....................................

ADDRESS...

CITY.......................................STATE.............Zip Code...........

TELEPHONE..AREA CODE:...............

NO ENTRY WILL BE ACCEPTED UNLESS THIS FORM IS SIGNED BY THE EXHIBITOR OR HIS AUTHORIZED AGENT. CHECKS FOR ENTRY FEE, AND STALL RENT, MUST ACCOMPANY ENTRIES. (NO EXHIBIT NUMBER DEPOSIT.)

Make checks payable to CALIFORNIA STATE HORSEMEN'S ASSOCIATION and mail, with entry blank to MRS. MARIE J. KEMM, 30 Martin Lane, Woodside, Calif. 94062 Phone (Area 415) 851-1557 After 6:30 P.M. Weekdays

ENTRY BLANK FOR SPRING CREEK FARM
OPEN HORSE SHOW
SATURDAY, APRIL 26 AND SUNDAY, APRIL 27, 1969
ENTRIES CLOSE APRIL 22, 1969

ENTRY FEES:
Classes - 11-12-16-18-30-33-36-40 - $10.00. All Others - $4.00
Post Entry Penalties: Trophy and Ribbon Classes - $1.00 / Stake Classes $2.00.

ENTRY FEES MUST ACCOMPANY ENTRIES

Make Checks Payable To: SPRING CREEK FARM and Mail To:
MRS. GAY PIPER, 24977 PALOMARES RD., HAYWARD, CA. 94546'
(415) 538-6311

CLASS	HORSE	RIDER	OWNER	FEE
			TOTAL	

RELEASE

I hereby release the Spring Creek Farm and its owners and employees of and from all claims which may hereafter develop or accrue to me on account of, or by reason of, any injury, loss or damage, which may be suffered by me, or to any property, because of any matter, thing or condition, negligence or default whatsoever, and I hereby assume and accept the full risk and danger of any hurt, injury or damage which may occur through or by reason of any matter, thing or condition, negligence or default, of any person or persons whatsoever.

Name _____ Address _____

City _____ State _____ Phone _____

I hereby consent to the entry of my child in the Spring Creek Farm Horse Show.

Juniors - Birth Date _____   _____
                                                               Signature of Parent or Guardian

The next one is for the California State Horsemen's show. This one has a release clause as do the others shown, except this first. In addition to the release clause, there is a statement that the exhibitor will abide by the rules of the American Horse Shows Association and the rules and regulations of the show. In all shows sanctioned by AHSA, the prospective contestant must acknowledge he and his horse are eligible to compete and will be bound by the AHSA rules.

A release clause, or hold harmless clause, is almost always a part of an entry blank. It does have a deterring action on exhibitors and makes them more careful. However, it does not relieve the show management from being careful. In case of any accident due to the negligence of the show management, the release clause will not cover them nor protect them from legal action due to carelessness.

The size of these entry forms is 8½" by 11", regular loose-leaf notebook size. They can have holes punched in ahead of time or done when the entry is returned.

APPENDIX C
PROGRAM FORMS

The following program pages show the method of handling classes, the sponsors, the specifications, the prize money if any, and the spacing for the results.

The first shown is from the 1966 California State Fair Horse Show. The second is from the 1968 California State Horsemen's Association Championship Horse Show.

The third example is a page from the exhibitors' list, a part of the 1966 program mentioned above. All large shows will have a list of the horses shown and their

WEDNESDAY AFTERNOON, JUNE 15—Continued

EVENT 6
Pacific Coast Hunter, Jumper and Stock Horse Association High Point Trail Horse Awards

CHAMPION. TRAIL HORSE_____

RESERVE CHAMPION TRAIL HORSE_____

EVENT 7
Class 76 — Stock Horses, Mares
Open to mares only and to be shown at a walk, jog trot and lope without restraint; lope a figure eight; run at speed; stop and turn easily. To be judged on cow work 50 points; rein 50 points; conformation 20 points; manners 20 points and appointments 10 points.

FIRST PRIZE: $45; 2nd, $35; 3rd, $20; 4th, $15; 5th, $10.

Class Sponsored by Mr. and Mrs. Alan Boland

323	Fillinic—Greg Ward	Greg Ward
601	Miss Hoodles—Linda Baker	Jack Baker
674	Booger's Bet—Linda Mitchell	Homer Mitchell
839	Lady Clabber—Linda Baker	Mr. & Mrs. Robert G. Haley
1305	Miss Freddy—Harry Rose	Harry Rose

1._____ 2._____ 3._____ 4._____ 5._____

EVENT 8
Class No. 83 — The Rainbo Baking Company
$500 Hackamore Horse Championship Stake
To be eligible horses must have been entered, shown and judged in any other class in this division. To be judged on cow work 50 points; rein 50 points; conformation 20 points; manners 20 points and appointments 10 points.

FIRST PRIZE: $100 and Trophy; 2nd, $85; 3rd, $70; 4th, $55; 5th, $45; 6th, $35; 7th, $30; 8th, $30; 9th, $25; 10th, $25.

Winner to Receive the T. H. Ramsey Memorial Trophy.

This trophy is competed for annually in memory of Mr. T. H. Ramsay who was a California State Fair Director and Chairman of the Horse Show Committee for many years. Suitable trophy to be given each year.

Won in 1940—Buddy, owned by H. Moffatt Co.
    1941—Jacinto, owned by H. Moffatt Co.
    1947—Benita, owned by Don Dodge
    1948—Tom Cat, owned by Don Dodge
    1949—Concho, owned by Reed H. McAllister
    1950—Dr. Maizie, owned by W. M. Howard
    1951—Dr. Maizie, owned by W. M. Howard
    1952—Brass Jr., owned by Juanita Frankini
    1953—Brass Jr., owned by Juanita Frankini
    1954—Shorty's Billie Joe, owned by Mr. and Mrs. Guy M. Corpe
    1955—Gin Fiz, owned by Lola Galli
    1956—Tomahawk, owned by R. D. Lohrman
    1957—Joe Queen, owned by Audie Murphy
    1958—Eddie Reed, owned by Mrs. Robert Cullman
    1959—Jernigan Peake, owned by William D. Dana
    1960—Fiddle D'Or, owned by Mr. and Mrs. Homer Mitchell
    1961—Right Now, owned by Mr. and Mrs. Vernon Vicini
    1962—Star Poco, Jim, owned by Bar D Quarter Horse Ranch
    1963—Night Mist, owned by William D. Dana
    1964—Bueno Buzz Bomb, owned by Frank J. Dutra
    1965—Pretty Pico, owned by Frank J. Dutra

103	Marco Tivio—Don Dodge	Ken Sutton
278	Sunny Star Bomb—Bobby Ingersoll	Mr. & Mrs. Meade Simpson
293	Poco Star Twinky—Bill Cochrane	Mr. & Mrs. W. T. Cochrane
326	Bar Lucky Seven—Greg Ward	Greg Ward
533	Ribbonette—Ray Hunt	Blenda Lewis
744	Chief—Frank Rue	Frank Rue
802	Kemo Sabey—Marvin Fayfield	Marvin Mayfield Stables
1057	Bull Parker—Jim Paul	Cecil M. Norris
1303	Deuce Reed—Bobby Ingersoll	David James
1306	Cattabar—Harry Rose	Homer Forrest
1307	Baby Come On—Harry Rose	Ginger Crowley

1.____ 2.____ 3.____ 4.____ 5.____ 6.____ 7.____ 8.____ 9.____ 10.____

EVENT 9
Pacific Coast Hunter, Jumper and Stock Horse Association High Point Hackamore Horse Awards

CHAMPION HACKAMORE HORSE_____

RESERVE CHAMPION HACKAMORE HORSE_____

WEDNESDAY EVENING, JUNE 15
7:30 P.M. — Main Arena

EVENT 1
Class 73 — Jumpers, Fault and Out
Minimum weight 165 pounds (154 pounds for women and juniors). To be shown over as many obstacles as may be jumped in one minute. Jumps to be from 4' to 4'6" in height with spreads from " to 6'. Points are awarded instead of faults (two points for each obstacle jumped clean and one point for the obstacle knocked down). The winner is the horse scoring the largest number of points with time to decide in the event of equality of points. Table II, Sec. 4(b). Touches not to count. Full point class.

Out of each entry fee $10 added and divided: 1st, 30%; 2nd, 25%; 3rd, 20%; 4th, 15%; 5th, 10%.

FIRST PRIZE: $45; 2nd, $35; 3rd, $20; 4th, $15; 5th, $10.

Class Sponsored by the Lorimer Stables, Oakland, California

345	Tally Ho—Stephanie Lloyd	Dr. & Mrs. R. C. Lawson
357	Eldorado—Rosita Pellas	Rosita Pellas
359	Sad Affair—Aljean Larson	Fiddlestix Farm
397	Plutonium—Gay Piper	Mr. & Mrs. Paul Piper
706	Munnings—Jim Kohn	Berry Hill Farm
711	Red Bank—Aljean Larson	Mr. & Mrs. Don Larson
797	Easy Street—Pat Blakiston	P and J Blakiston
884	On the Wing—Champ Hough	Mr. & Mrs. Champ Hough
934	High Mr. Pop-Over—Phyllis Cetti	High Riders Jumping Club
1113	Granny Goose—Suzanna Willoughby	Zaccalini and Willoughby
1144	Special Tithe—Judy Benz	Judith Benz
1151	Dutch Treat—Jim Kohn	Col. Alex Sysin
1188	Book Learnin'—Gene Lewis	Westoak Farm
1218	Kid Shannon—Ken Nordstrom	Mr. & Mrs. Jimmy Williams
1221	High Hopes—Marcia Williams	Mr. & Mrs. Jimmy Williams
1222	Circus Wonder—Marcia Williams	Mrs. Alan Boland
1230	Little Jen—Jimmy Williams	Mr. & Mrs. M. W. Brickman
1231	Golden Rule—Denise Beck	Mr. & Mrs. M. W. Brickman
1260	Spitt-n-Image—Barbara Oakford	R. Mitchel McClure
1261	Ben Casey—Barbara Oakford	R. Mitchel McClure
1262	Golden Stirrups—Cindy Dodge	Cortesia Cadillac
1278	Windy Lee—Barbara Oakford	Courtesy Chevrolet
1279	Filthy Sullivan—Barbara Oakford	Courtesy Chevrolet
1330	Medicine Man—Ronnie Freeman	Al Davis.
1331	Ivar—Ronnie Freeman	Robert E. Freeman
1333	Pardon Me—Ronnie Freeman	Ronald G. Freeman

1.____ 2.____ 3.____ 4.____ 5.____

EVENT 2
Class 38 — Harness Ponies, Amateur to Drive
Ponies to show all-around action at a park pace and not faster. To be driven in the half cheek, appear to have perfect mouths, should stand quietly, remaining checked while lined up; and back easily. To be judged on manners, quality and performance.

FIRST PRIZE: $45; 2nd, $35; 3rd, $20; 4th, $15; 5th, $10.

Trophy Sponsored by Sacramento County Board of Supervisors

223	King's Sweet Rhythm—Mrs. William P. Roth	Mrs. William P. Roth
851	Jubilee's Danny Dee—Mrs. John Pritzlaff	Mrs. John C. Pritzlaff, Jr.
1024	Charming Acres Minstrel—Julie Hawley	Julie Hawley
1129	Holiday Cheer—Alice Ruth Woolsey	Alice Ruth Woolsey
1133	Mary Poppin—Patricia Holmes	The Unicorn Farm

1.____ 2.____ 3.____ 4.____ 5.____

EVENT 3
Class 7 — Five-Gaited Saddle Horses, Open
To be shown at a walk, trot, slow gait, rack and canter. To be judged on performance, quality and manners.

FIRST PRIZE: $45; 2nd, $35; 3rd, $20; 4th, $15; 5th, $10.

Class Sponsored by Bank of Sacramento

212	Precious Trust—James Koller	Mrs. William P. Roth
848	Festival—Linda Briggs	Mr. & Mrs. Ronald Antonioli
944	Maple Miracle—Mrs. Roy Robinson	Maple Stables
946	Maple Marengo—Mrs. Robinson	Maple Stables
1176	Little Caesar—Mrs. R. D. Zapp	Vagabond Stables
1315	Mr. Peacock—Buddy Shay	Jack Edwards
1352	Holiday Playboy—V. C. Adams	Paul B. Cannon

1.____ 2.____ 3.____ 4.____ 5.____

EVENT 4
Parade of Stallions

Friday Afternoon, August 23   Cypress Ring, Event 3

Class No. 79 — Stock Seat Equitation Championship - Riders 17 and Under

To be judged on seat, hands, performance of horse and appointments of horse and rider. Individual performance is required of all contestants.

Sponsored by—REDWOOD RANGERS DRIVING & RIDING CLUB

73	SUGAR RAY—Debbie Caselli	Debra Caselli
126	CAMEO GINA—Carol Jung	Carol Jung
168	SALTY BRITCHES—Claire Lund	Claire Lund
176	POKEY'S ROGUE—Debbie Bryant	R. A. Bryant
199	TUCKER—Kathy Blackford	Miss Pat Greene Mayhew
208	NIGHT QUEST—Chris Salyer	Marian Salyer
212	GOLDIE AGAR—Arlene Kimura	Frank Kimura
216	LUCKY PENNY—Edie Strain	Frederick Strain
252	LUCKY CINNAMON—Judy Costa	Mr. & Mrs. Frank Costa, Jr.
264	BAR REX—Debbie Baumer	Debbie Baumer
265	RODIE—Shellie Baumer	Shellie Baumer
267	SHERRI—Gary Baumer	Gary Baumer
274	ZIPPER—Bubbles Solum	Rod Kelly
294	TIPPY'S MARK—Nancy Rowe	Maynard Missal
313	REDWOOD RUTH—"Dez" Golden	Carousel Stables
322	DUNDEE—Cheryl Bradley	Kathy Hudson
332	CASINO ROYAL—Jackie Lundy	Jackelyn Lundy
386	DONNIE TOP—B. J. Henning	B. J. & L. A. Henning
395	KING'S RITA—Carole Neely	R. J. Neely
427	TONTO'S JOHN—Lori Cornell	Lori Cornell
430	ZINGO—Ed Randolph	Erle Randolph
506	SHIRLEY CHEX—Virginia Haley	Katherine H. Haley
510	SIERRA ROXANNE—Kelly Hemphell	Jack Hemphell
548	AARON CHIQUITH—Dee Dee Simmons	Dee Dee Simmons
573	MUSIC GAL—Kent Kramer	Joan Stege
578	SNIPPER'S BOBBY—Jon Kerr	Dr. and Mrs. Rees
580	BRANDY—Sheila Kelley	Rod Kelley

1st	2nd	3rd	4th	5th
6th	7th	8th	9th	10th

Friday Evening, August 23   Beck Arena, Event 4

Class No. 120 — Senior Drill Teams

To be judged on horses 90 pts., equipment 60 pts., uniforms 60 pts., and drill 790 pts., under C.S.H.A. rules.
THE SENIOR DRILL TEAM WILL DRILL IMMEDIATELY BEFORE EVENT NO. 3.

SACRAMENTO COUNTY SHERIFF'S MOUNTED POSSE

Friday Evening, August 23   Beck Arena, Event 1

Class No. 27 — Jumpers - Amateur Owner to Ride

To be shown over nine jumps 3'6" to 4' in height with a spread of 4' to 5'. In event of equality of faults, successive jump-offs will count. Table I. Touches to count. Prize Money $50.00.

Sponsored by—DR. AND MRS. DONALD Q. STRUTKER.

7	LITTLE BIG JOHN—Val Tohill	Bedlam Acres
130	THE KOPPER KAT—Mrs. D. Smith	Mrs. D. Smith
155	CANUCK—Susan Higley	Susan Higley
156	GARYOWEN—Vince Giese	Giese Realty
176	SHAMROCK—Cheryl Kronlund	Cheryl Kronlund
188	TEXAS RASCAL—Judy Pearson	Judy Rae Pearson
380	TINFOIL—John Vogley	John N. Vogley
396	NEVADA LOUIE—Phyllis Cetti	Mr. & Mrs. Leo Cetti
433	MERLIN—Rosita Pellas	Rosita Pellas
614	DR. GAINES—Tim Wright	Fox Tail Farm
618	SILK N SATIN—Pat Crowe	Four Winds Farm
622	MR. COMPLETELY—Sue Pearson	Shadow Valley Farm
630	FANCY PANTS—Richard Schulke	Richard Schulke

1st	2nd	3rd	4th
5th	6th	7th	8th

Friday Evening, August 23   Beck Arena, Event 2

Class No. 18 — Working Hunters, Regular - Open

To be judged on performance and soundness. Fences 4'. Prize Money $125.00.

Sponsored by — DR. AND MRS. THEODORE STASHAK.

11	TRICK OR TREAT—Brooke Stevens	Mrs. William Halford, Jr.
46	RASH MOMENT—Richard Keller	Oakhill Acres

48	MICHO ARLEN—Jackie Hamilton	Jackie Hamilton
49	GREEN BRIAR—Robin Postmanter	Robin Postmanter
51	WELLS FARGO—Robin Postmanter	Ingrid Jansen
61	GILROY—Richard "Dick" Keller	Kris Hartje
100	SANTA CRUZ—Kris Smith	Mr. & Mrs. Jerrold Smith
123	SORCERER'S APPRENTICE—Teri Saunders	Marty Strasburg
132	THE IVORY KNIGHT—Margaret Ferrari	Margaret Ferrari
146	GALLANT GUY—Gay Piper	Alexis Milton
183	THE PERFECTIONIST—Linda Kibbee	Mary Beth Kirk
184	THUMBS UP—Linda Kibbee	Jarvis Esedwein
202	WHO—Stephanie Lloyd	Larry Lloyd Stables
232	SALONGA CARRIER—Kathy Lutz	Idle Acres
235	BIG DEAL—Lynn Thomas	Lynn Thomas
250	"AFTER DARK"—Peggy Bobb	Peggy Bobb
324	TRIUMPH V.—Vicki Olsen	Harold Swoverland
331	AFTER SIX—Tom Kay	Berry Hill Farm, Inc.
340	PLEASE REPEAT—Harry Burkett	Foxfield
380	TINFOIL—John Vogley	John N. Vogley
381	DIVINE TIME—John Vogley	John N. Vogley,
421	GAKAN—Maureen Haley	Mr. & Mrs. Wm. D. Haley
433	MERLIN—Rosita Pellas	Rosita Pellas
555	HUNT MASTER—Larry Mayfield	F-V Podesta Farms
559	INSTANT TROUBLE—Linda Lorimer	Laura Davies
561	MAKE BELIEVE—Linda Lorimer	Mr. & Mrs. Paul L. Davies, Jr.
604	TUCUMCARI—Stephanie Dishal	Carillon Farms
614	DR. GAINES—Tim Wright	Fox Tail Farm
615	LORD BELN—Tim Wright	Fox Tail Farm
618	SILK N SATIN—Pat Crowe	Four Winds Farm
622	MR. COMPLETELY—Sue Pearson	Shadow Valley Farm

1st	2nd	3rd	4th
5th	6th	7th	8th

Friday Evening, August 23   Back Arena, Event 3

Class No. 51 — English Pleasure Horse Championship, Hunter Type - Riders 17 and Under

To be shown at a walk, trot and canter both ways of the ring. To be judged on manners, quality and performance.

Sponsored by—SAN MATEO COUNTY HORSEMEN'S ASSOCIATION

CLASS NO. 51 WILL BE JUDGED IN SECTIONS A and B.

A	6	IRISH TENOR—Kathy Tohill	Bedlam Acres
B	17	SONNY SHOES—Judie Wertheim	Fred Wertheim
A	18	ORBIT—Lisa Weissich	Lisa Weissich
B	21	VEGAS CHANCE—Buffie Hicks	Buhy Shields
A	22	A PATCH OF BLUE—Laurie Mactavish	Laurie Mactavish
B	23	ROYAL MARINER—Robyn Williams	Robyn Williams
A	24	HOLLY GOLIGHTLY—Margaret Daly	Mr. & Mrs. R.J. Daly
B	25	AMELIA C—Allison Rollins	Allison Rollins
A	26	NEXTAN—Marguerite DiGiorgio	Marguerite DiGiorgio
B	32	FRIENDLY PERSUASION—Susette Roemer	Susette Roemer
A	33	BLUE ANGEL—Brenda Roemer	Brenda Roemer
B	35	COUNTRY MILE—Diana Hanson	Diana Hanson
A	36	BRIGHT FUTURE—Odette Solon	Mr. & Mrs. G. K. Solon
B	38	HURRY BACK—Barbara Horsell	Barbara Horsell
A	41	99-E—Lois Yaffee	W. Yaffee
B	50	CAREFULL KATY—Joan Schwartz	Joan Schwartz
A	51	WELLS FARGO—Debbie Beamer	Ingrid Jansen
B	59	HECTOR—Coco Wendling	Foxfield
A	61	GILROY—Kris Hartje	Kris Hartje
B	82	LEISURE TIME—Pam Brown	Ivan B. Brown
A	89	ANGUS MC DUFF—Jan Paden	Dr. Wm. W. Paden
B	105	AFTERMATH—Jennifer McCune	Aromas Hills Farms
A	145	BANTER—Celeste Milton	Spring Creek Farm
B	146	GALLANT GUY—Alexis Milton	Alexis Milton
A	200	OUT OF PRINT—Marie Cote'	Larry Lloyd Stables
B	206	PATEND PENDING—Mary Reese	Mrs. Margaret E. Reese
A	231	NORTHQUEST—Kathy Lutz	Idle Acres
B	269	MARZY DOATS—Jan Toth	Jan Toth
A	289	GALLANT BATTLER—Teri Saunders	Teri Saunders
B	300	GRAND TOIL—Marva Mayfield	Marvin Mayfield
A	326	BUFFY—Diane Resetar	Diane Resetar
B	328	GARDEN PRINCE—Kathy Graver	Graver Farms
A	333	TOURIST—Mary Ahnlund	Carol Ahnlund
B	338	SUMMERTIME—Heidi Davis	Heidi Davis
A	529	RED SABU—Nancy Witter	T. W. Witter
B	536	HAWK—Lynn Leatham	Kimberwicke Farms
A	539	COOKSON KID—Missy Murray	Missy Murray
B	540	HONOR BRIGHT—Susan Leatham	Kimberwicke Farms
A	550	HARBOR LIGHTS—Robin de la Ossa	Robin Del Farms
B	556	SUNSHINE BRIAN—Irene Lorimer	Irene Lorimer
A	557	MIGHTY WIZARD—Celia Lorimer	Celia Lorimer
B	560	SILLER—Laura Davies	Laura Davies
A	606	INDIAN ROYALTY—Lisa Bettini	Lisa Bettini
B	617	POWER PAK—Douglas Day	Douglas Day

1st	2nd	3rd	4th	5th
6th	7th	8th	9th	10th

1st	2nd	3rd	4th	5th
6th	7th	8th	9th	10th

HORSES AND THEIR EXHIBITORS — Continued

180 Gambler's Gold, Pal G, 15.1, 8....Susan Griggs, Rancho Cordova
181 Helmaur Graceful
Gr. M, 12.1, 6..........Mr. & Mrs. James W. Taylor, Carmichael
182 Entry, Gr S..............Mr. & Mrs. James W. Taylor, Carmichael
183 Produce of Dam..........Mr. & Mrs. James W. Taylor, Carmichael
184 Graceful's Buckaroo
Gr S, 1.......Mr. & Mrs. Russell Deterding, Jr., Carmichael
185 Indian Mule
App G, 15.3, A..........Mr. & Mrs. Richard Burton, Sacramento
186 Lost Fiddle, B M, 15, 3..........Mrs. Charles Greene, Sacramento
187 Bev-a-lan Folly, Gr M, 3.......Mr. & Mrs. Alan Thayer, Grimes
188 Knobby Knolls Cimerron
Gr G, 4.............................Mr. & Mrs. Alan Thayer, Grimes
189 JSCO Golden King, Pal G, 8....Mr. & Mrs. Alan Thayer, Grimes
190 Sundowner's Gypsy
App M, 53" 4......................Clarence & Grace Sykes, Oakdale
191 Fox Snowflake, App S, 52, 9....Clarence & Grace Sykes, Oakdale
192 Ko Ko Lynn
Bay M, 15.1, 6.......Charley & J. R. Murphey, Bellevue, Wash.
193 Zadi Fe, Bay S, 14.1, 6.............................Bell Bar Ranch, Auburn
194 Rogues Rebel, C S, 14.2, 4....Irwin & Margaret Froman, Ontario
195 Mar-win Lazy Mac
C S, 14.2, 2..........................Irwin & Margaret Froman, Ontario
196 Mar-win Sue Juana
C M, 14.2, 3.......................Irwin & Margaret Froman, Ontario
197 Troopers "Mr. Ready-Go"
Bl M, 15.2, 3................Mr. & Mrs. James A. Bourland, Fontana
198 Take Em Again, Ch M, 12.1, 1.......Kathy Cromwell, Woodside
199 Dandy Music, Sor G, 15.1, 6.......................Laura Kerns, Nicolaus
200 Red Rambler, Ch S, 15.1, 5.......James & Dee Paloneni, Elverta
201 High 'N Wise
Br G, 16.1, 7.......Continental Trailer Parks, Rolling Hills Est.
202 Jack Daniel, App S, 15.2, 5.......................Gordon H. Smith, Lakeport
203 Strutter's Top
Dap S, 43½", 3..........Al & Audrey Richardson, Walnut Creek
204 Uptown Strutter
Ch S, 45¾", 3..............Al & Audrey Richardson, Walnut Creek
205 Hash's Royal Angel
Ch M, 41, 5......................Al & Audrey Richardson, Walnut Creek
206 Merry Harvest Chief
Rn G, 15.3, 4................Richard N. Leamon, West Sacramento
207 Little Eli, Rn G, 14.2, 2....Richard N. Leamon, West Sacramento
208 Leisure Bay, Bay G, 16.1, 6...........Fiddlestix Farms, Grass Valley
209 Macadam, Blk G, 16.2, 6.......................Mrs. Bess Cassidy, Stockton
210 Nite Witch, Blk M, 15, 7.......................Cathy Dodge, Sacramento
211 Patrick Rhythm, Ch G, 16.2, 4....Mrs. William P. Roth, San Mateo
212 Precious Trust, Bay M, 15.3, 7....Mrs. William P. Roth, San Mateo
213 Whyworry Reflection
Ch M, 16, 5..............................Mrs. William P. Roth, San Mateo
214 Revel Tree, Ch G, 16, A..........Mrs. William P. Roth, San Mateo
215 Rhythm's Jewel, Blk M, 16, 4....Mrs. William P. Roth, San Mateo
216 Whyworry Blackbird
Ch M, 16, 3..............................Mrs. William P. Roth, San Mateo
217 Magic Fern, Bay M, 12.3, 7.......Mrs. William P. Roth, San Mateo
218 Whyworry Prima Donna
Bay M, 12, 9..............................Mrs. William P. Roth, San Mateo
219 Whyworry Brigadoon
Brn G, 13.1½, 8..................Mrs. William P. Roth, San Mateo
220 Kenwil Lady Hollie
Bay M, 13, A..........................Mrs. William P. Roth, San Mateo
221 Whyworry Dazzelier
Bay M, 12.3½, 6......................Mrs. William P. Roth, San Mateo
222 Tamerlane's Cadet Kathleen
Bay M, 47¼", 5........................Mrs. William P. Roth, San Mateo
223 King's Sweet Rhythm
Bl M, 12.1¾, A........................Mrs. William P. Roth, San Mateo
224 Whyworry Flame
Bay M, 12¾, 4.........................Mrs. William P. Roth, San Mateo
225 Silver Field, Gr S, 15.2, A.......Mrs. William P. Roth, San Mateo
226 Pat Alden, Bay G, 16, 5............Mrs. William P. Roth, San Mateo
227 Stately's Fair Chance
Sor S, 14, 1...............................Ruth R. Christman, Fair Oaks
228 Ruff's 2 x 4
App S, 2....Conrad Ruff Estate & Ernestene Ruff, Marysville
229 Ruff's Chuck
App S, 1....Conrad Ruff Estate & Ernestene Ruff, Marysville
230 Ruff's Jewel
App M.......Conrad Ruff Estate & Ernestene Ruff, Marysville
231 Ruff's Ginger
App M, 1....Conrad Ruff Estate & Ernestene Ruff, Marysville
232 Ruff's Running Star
App M, 15, 4..............Conrad Ruff Estate & Ernestene Ruff
Marysville
233 Get of Sire.......Conrad Ruff Estate & Ernestene Ruff, Marysville
234 Produce of Dam
Conrad Ruff Estate & Ernestene Ruff, Marysville
235 Oak Bar's Punkin.......................Hugh Kolowich, Jr., Atherton
236 Top Rooster, Bay G, 15.3, 3.........................Betty Rutz, Nicolaus
237 Ping Pong, Sor M, 14.3, 9....................Susan Lawton, Santa Ana
238 Crosswood Sensation
Ch G, 17, 6...................Mrs. Richard Briggs, Citrus Heights
239 William G., Ch G, 14.3, A.......................Henry N. Bakken, Stockton
240 Lorenzo, Pal G, 15.3, 5.............................Linda Doyle, Carmichael
241 Secret's Mary Legs, Bl M, 16, 4................Frances North, Camino
242 Miss Merry Trouble, Ch M, 15.1, 4............Frances North, Camino
243 Our Blooming Heir, Ro G, 15.2, 6..............Frances North, Camino
244 Candlelight, Pal G, 16, 7.........................Julie Graham, Sacramento
245 Sho Shawnee's Sierra Sam
App ML, 1 Mo........................Larry Donaldson, Citrus Heights
246 Ahnakea's Miss Blue
Sp M, 15.2, 3...............Betsy Walbridge, Wickenburg, Ariz.
247 Leona's Folly
Sor M, 15.2, 3...........................Betsy Walbridge, Wickenburg, Ariz.
248 Mr. Smokey Bars, Dun S, 13.2, 1...........Dick Vaughn, San Jose
249 Treasure V Bay, Bay G, 15, 4....Robert & Loretta Smith, Live Oak
250 Cavalier King Larigo
Sp S, 44", 4..............................Joyce & James R. Lipsett, Oroville
251 Circle L M Flash's Dan Patch
Sor S, 41, 1..............................Joyce & James R. Lipsett, Oroville
252 Happyland's Charming Valerie
Br M, 42" 4..............................Joyce & James R. Lipsett, Oroville
253 Phil's Royal Surprise
Ch M, 40, 1..............................Joyce & James Lipsett, Oroville
254 Sterling Star Philibuster
Ch S, 41, 5..............................Joyce & James R. Lipsett, Oroville
255 Gallant Battler, Ch G, 15.3, 6.......Teri Eugenia Saunders, Danville
256 Miss Muffet, Ch G, 15, 8..........Teri Eugenia Saunders, Danville
257 Royal Amber, Ch S, 1..................................Marvin L. Garrett, Ceres
258 Lady Amber, Ch M, 2..................................Marvin L. Garrett, Ceres
259 Be Bop, Bl M, 15, A...Shelley Hughes, Visalia
260 China Doll, Pn M, 15, 6...Shelley Hughes, Visalia
261 Heart Throb, Bay G, 16.2, 8....Mr. & Mrs. I. McAlister, Sacramento
262 Misfit, Ch G, 16, 8...................Mr. & Mrs. I. McAlister, Sacramento
263 Hammon's Keno
Bl S, 46" 6......................E. W. & Florence Rossberg, Manteca
264 Miracle's Shadow
Bl M, 48¼, 2....................E. W. & Florence Rossberg, Manteca
265 Chan's Sparkette, App G, 15, 6..............Suzanne M. Mell, Salinas
266 Lady Wampum, Ch M, 15.1, A..............Suzanne M. Mell, Salinas
267 Chargeono Bar, App S, 14.1, 2..............Suzanne M. Mell, Salinas
268 Taffy, Ch M, 15, 7...Marcia Blumer, Orinda
269 Domino Reed, B G, 16, 7.....................................Marcia Blumer, Orinda
270 Script T Tequila, Ch M, 1..............Ruth Kline Tollefson, Toledo
271 Script T Mountain Dew, Bay Fe, 1....Ruth Kline Tollefson, Toledo
272 Script T Daiquiri, Rn Fe, 3..............Ruth Kline Tollefson, Toledo
273 Produce of Dam..................................Ruth Kline Tollefson, Toledo
274 Get of Sire..Ruth Kline Tollefson, Toledo
275 Tanglewood Spring Lights Lady
Bay Fe..Ruth Kline Tollefson, Toledo
276 Red Mesa, Ch G, 14.3, 7...................Sharon R. Joyner, Sacramento
277 Beau Chanson, Br G, 17.1, 6...........Cherril Young, Redwood City
278 Sunny Star Bomb
Bay M, 15, 5..................................Mr. & Mrs. Meade Simpson, Hood
279 Miladye Midnight, Ch M, 15.1, 8.....................Ann Clark, Saratoga
280 Miss Jupiter, Ch M, 15.2, A.......................John A. Craggs, Fair Oaks
281 Mac's Chinook, Ch S, 15, 5...........Gerald C. McDonnell, Stockton
282 Lady Fiona, Bay M, 14, 2...............Gerald C. McDonnell, Stockton
283 Fenraw's Amber, Ch M, 16, 5..................Fenraw Farm, Riverside
284 Saracen Trooper, Ch S, 15.3, 3..............Fenraw Farm, Riverside
285 Boss Man, Sor G, 16, A.........................Christine Bogs, Lafayette
286 The Royal Tartan of River's Crest
Ch S, 3...River's Crest Stables, Santa Cruz
287 River's Crest Gingham Lass
Sp M, 1...River's Crest Stables, Santa Cruz
288 River's Crest Valiant, Gr S, 3....River's Crest Stables, Santa Cruz
289 Get of Sire...............................River's Crest Stables, Santa Cruz
290 Produce of Dam..........................River's Crest Stables, Santa Cruz
291 Phantom Beau
Ch G, 15.3, 4..........Richard & Deanne Johnson, Orangevale
292 Teresa Q Mark, Sor M, 15, 6....Walter Sanders, Walnut Creek
293 Poco Star Twinky
Sor M, 14.3, 4.................Mr. & Mrs. W. T. Cochrane, Salinas
294 Hardesty's Flash Luke
Sor S, 41, 2..................................Hardesty's Pony Farm, Chico
295 Bay Flash, Bay S, 3.......................Hardesty's Pony Farm, Chico
296 King Wild Fire Danny Boy
S, 1...Hardesty's Pony Farm, Chico
297 Fancy Fashion Hillswicke
Bay M, 44, 4.................................Hardesty's Pony Farm, Chico
298 Nancy's Pepper, Sor M, 42, 3.......Hardesty's Pony Farm, Chico
299 Get of Sire...................................Hardesty's Pony Farm, Chico
300 Produce of Dam...........................Hardesty's Pony Farm, Chico
301 Shadel Tirzsh
Ch M, 14.2, 5.......Mmes. Jo-Ann L. & H. W. Klein, Vacaville
302 Deacon's Annie, B M, 14.2, 1......................William H. Neel, Davis
303 Maria's Deacon, S S, 15.3, 5......................William H. Neel, Davis
304 Nina, Bl M, 15, A...Pamela Sprague, Sacramento
305 Morada's Gay Boy, Ch G, 15½, A........Frank Peterson, Stockton
306 Wilson's Tam, Bay M, 15.2, 4....Donna Rae Bedient, Wheatland
307 Van's Comet, Ch F, 14.1, 2..................C. R. Vandercook, Arcadia
308 Don's Bonnie Lu
Ch M, 14.3, 4......................Don & Loretta Breazeale, Modesto
309 Loridon Princess Dee
Ch M, 14, 2..........................Don & Loretta Breazeale, Modesto
310 S R Perfect Dawn, Gr F, 14.3, 6..............Ona Mae Hale, San Jose
311 Stony Ridge Maiden
Rn F, 48", 3.......Marlin & Lucellle Noble, Burlington, Wash.
312 Gordon's Flash
Pal S, 15, 2..............Roy L. & Lorene E. Gordon, Brentwood
313 Smokey Pistol, Sor G, 15, A..............Betty J. Pinto, El Sobrante
314 Doc's Kona Bar, Ch M, 13, 1..................Francis Grupe, Linden
315 Fresno Rogue Fox, Ch G, 15.1, 4............Francis Grupe, Linden
316 Bay State Ideal, Bay S, 14.3¾, 5..............John & Polly Bee, Ojai
317 Bay State Bonnie, Bay M, 15, A..............John & Polly Bee, Ojai
318 Long Hill Toralenda, Bay M, 15.1, 3......John & Polly Bee, Ojai
319 Matilija Fawn-Danna, Bay M, 14.3, 2.......John & Polly Bee, Ojai
320 Shackle Lee, Br G, 16.3, 5..................Georgene Dovolis, Monterey
321 Sunny Robin, Ch M, 14.3, 3..................James E. Miller, Carmichael
322 Sho Shawnee Tippy, Sor M, 13, 1....Loyd L. Johnson, Brisbane
323 Fillinic, Sor M, 14.2, 9..................................Greg Ward, Porterville
324 Little Echols, Sor G, 14.2, A........................Greg Ward, Porterville
325 Little Buck, Bu G, 14.2, 6.............................Greg Ward, Porterville
326 Lucky Seven, Sor G, 15.3, 4.........................Greg Ward, Porterville
327 Mister Grotchet...............................Walking-W Ranch, Sacramento
328 Shadow's Fire Cracker, S..............Walking-W Ranch, Sacramento
329 Chestnut Ridge..................................Walking-W Ranch, Sacramento
330 Ramblers Rouge, App G, 16.2, A...........Jackie Spiltnoff, Oakland
331 Fleet Victory, Bl M, 16.1, 8..................Miss Laura Davies, Oakland
332 Easter Bar, Bay G, 16.1, A.....................Barbara Horsell, Oakland
333 Robi Jonn..Barbara Horsell, Oakland
334 Tucumcari, Ch G, 16.1, A........................Stephanie Dishal, Oakland
335 Special Train, Br M, 16.2, 6................Mrs. Myron Jacobs, Oakland
336 Dance Music, Ch M, 16, A......................Mrs. Myron Jacobs, Oakland
337 Greenbriar, Br G, 16.2, A.......................Robin Posmanter, Oakland
338 Siller, Bay M, 16.3, 7................................Maggie Lorimer, Oakland
339 Just-A-Minute, Bay M, 15.1, A........Larry Lloyd Stables, Kenwood
340 Without Words, Ch M, 15.3, 3.........Larry Lloyd Stables, Kenwood
341 Full Cry, Bay G, 16.2, A......................Larry Lloyd Stables, Kenwood
342 Battle Steel, Bay M, 16.2, 7..................Larry Lloyd Stables, Kenwood
343 Court Squire, Ch G, 16.1, 4.................Larry Lloyd Stables, Kenwood
344 Arnad, Gr S, 15, 5...Sally Babson, Vallejo

owners. Many smaller affairs, not wanting the expense of a program, will use this prize list, supplementing it with a mimeographed sheet showing the horses and contestants.

APPENDIX D
HUNTER AND JUMPER COURSES
(PRIZE LIST)

It is customary for the premium list of a large affair to illustrate the hunter and jumper courses. Two examples are shown: the first from the 1969 California State Fair Horse Show and the other from the 1969 CSHA Championship Horse Show. In both cases, the designer was Col. Alex P. Sysin, the dean of designers on the West Coast and the 1958 winner of the Mr. and Mrs. Wm. C. Cox Trophy, awarded annually by the American Horse Shows Association for jumper course designing.

In the first example the arena was long enough but not as wide as could be desired. In the second, the arena was about 180′ x 280′, large enough for almost any kind of course.

Note that some courses were used for more than one class. In such cases, horses going in one of the classes would not be going in another class over the same course.

APPENDIX E
WORK SHEETS

Following is a work sheet that can be mimeographed on 8½″ x 11″ lightweight paper. The reason for light paper is that up to five copies will be needed, and the last carbon copy should be legible.

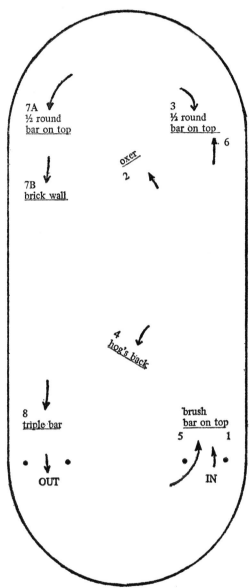

Sec. 60—Jumpers—Handy. Jumps four feet to four feet six inches; spreads five to six feet.

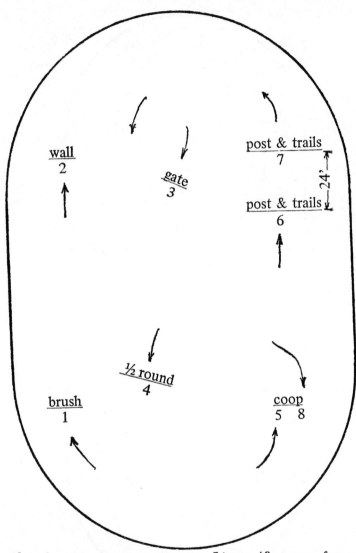

Class 3. GREEN WORKING HUNTERS—Livery (first year fences, 3′ 6″; second year fences, 3′ 9″).
Class 40. WORKING HUNTERS—Livery—Amateur Owner (fences 3′ 6″).

Of the copies made, one should go to the in gate man, one to the ringmaster, one to the ring secretary, one to the announcer, and one should be kept by the entry secretary.

When post entries are accepted, it is the show secretary who takes the entry. It is entered immediately on her copy, and then she must transmit the information to the ring secretary and the in gate man. The ring secretary adds the information to the ringmaster's and announcer's copies. If there are late scratches or absentees, the show secretary must get the message out to all concerned. Occasionally, the in gate man is the first to know of a late scratch, and he must get the word to the holders of the work sheets.

Holes may be punched in the work sheets for filing in a loose-leaf binder by the show secretary and ring secretary. The other copies will be either loose in hand or on a clipboard.

The sheet shown has room for 17 entries. Twenty is a better figure. The reason for this is that most classes with over 40 entries are usually split into two sections.

If it is a money class and the judge's signature is necessary, it can be obtained at a later time, rather than holding up the class while the judge checks from his card to the work sheet.

CLASS NO. ....

Prize Money	Award	Judged	Entry No.	Horse	Rider	Owner

IMPORTANT

No premiums may be paid until Judge's Certificate has been signed and the sheet has been signed and dated by the Judge's Clerk.

Date Judged ....19........

....
Judge's Clerk

JUDGE'S CERTIFICATE

I hereby certify that I have judged the entries listed above, ... in number, in accordance with the rules and regulations prescribed by the California State Horsemen's Association and the American Horse Shows Association and further certify that the placing has been made as noted thereon.

(Signed) ....
Judge

APPENDIX F
JUDGE'S CARDS

Two types of judge's cards are shown here. The larger one is 5½" by 11", and the smaller one is 5" by 8". These are printed on cardboard so that the judge can hold them in hand rather than use a clipboard.

In each case there is room on the upper part to place the class specifications. This is a great help to the judge so that he knows exactly what the exhibitors have entered and what they expect to be judged on.

The larger card is usually used at shows where the classes are not overly large. The show secretary may enter the numbers of the contestants on the card, but in large shows this is not feasible. So in most large shows the judge will use the smaller type of card for most classes on the flat, and the jumper card for hunters and jumpers. He can also use the two types in conjunction, making his final awards on the smaller.

Various types of cards can be ordered commercially from suppliers who advertise in the national and local horse magazines. If given a form to follow, a local printer can make these up as reasonably as possible by ordering them through a catalogue.

If you expect to run the placings as far down as the tenth, then when having the cards made up, specify this to the printer and he will take care of it.

HORSE SHOW JUDGES' SCORE CARD

HUNTERS AND JUMPERS

CONDITIONS

First............Second............Third............Fourth............Fifth............

Sixth............Reserve............ *Judges will select and mark "RESERVE" one more horse than the number of awards in any class to provide for the contingency of a disqualification.*

No.	1	2	3	4	5	6	7	8	9	10	Conformation	Manners and Way of Going	Performance	Total

SIGNED_____

Class No. ....

Event.

WINNERS

1. ....
2. ....
3. ....
4. ....
5. ....
6. ....
7. ....
8. ....
9. ....
10. ....

Judge ....

APPENDIX G
DESIGNING JUMPER COURSES

As stated before, designing jumper courses is an art. Although it can be taught by others and the basics can be learned from a book, the best teacher is actual experience. A person who has ridden many jumper courses has an excellent knowledge of what makes a fair course. He knows the average stride of a jumper, his arc when jumping, and the radius of his turns. These are all important considerations when drawing up a course.

A course designer will sketch out his courses, knowing what jumps he has available and the size of the arena. He can draw these courses from a premium list. But when he actually supervises the setting up of the course, he will walk from jump to jump, putting himself in the exhibitor's saddle, and visualizing each stride the horse will be taking. Then he will make sure the distances between jumps are right for the expected competition. For top horses and riders, these distances are varied to make the rider handle his mount with thought. Where the type of horse competing is average, the designer will lay out an average course.

Variety is the spice of life, so the saying goes. It is also the key to a good jump course. The day of four-post and rail jumps, twice around, has long gone. Most jumping class specifications call for at least eight jumps. These should all be different if possible. There will be times when a jump will have to be taken twice in the course of a round, but this should be avoided if it can be.

However, there are many small shows that are unable to own or borrow more than four, five, or six jumps. In such cases, there will be jumps that will have to be taken more than once. In these instances, that jump should be one that can be jumped from either direction. This makes the designing easier.

The American Horse Shows Association and the Federation Equestre Internationale give the heights, spreads, and number of jumps for each class included in their specification. Hence a wise course designer has a copy of these rules in hand when he is figuring out the courses. These rules will tell what jumps go to make up a combination, the distance between jumps when part of a combination, and how to measure these distances.

Any course in which time will be an element must be measured from the start to the finish. There are several ways to do this. One is to use a measuring wheel. Another way is to tape the distance with a 100-foot tape. One can pace it if he is certain of his stride. When using the latter method, it is best to pace the course at least twice and average the results.

When drawing up the course for the exhibitors, it is only necessary to show the jumps in the order they are to be taken and the direction in which they are to be jumped. When measuring the course one should consider the most obvious route that an exhibitor will take. There will be those with handy horses who will figure out ways to cut corners, but the person doing the measuring should take what route he considers the most likely to be used.

On the next few pages are shown some jump courses using less than the usual eight jumps. Also shown are a few with eight jumps. Where jumps are shown close together these are meant to be a combination. Since combinations are judged differently than single jumps, it is best to number each jump of the combination with the

JUMP COURSES USING FOUR JUMPS

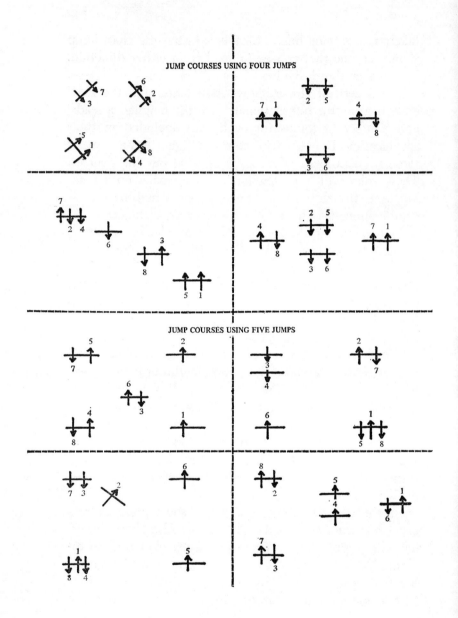

JUMP COURSES USING FIVE JUMPS

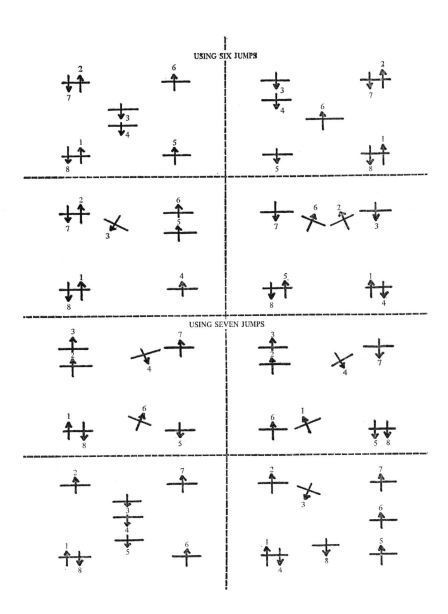

USING SEVEN JUMPS

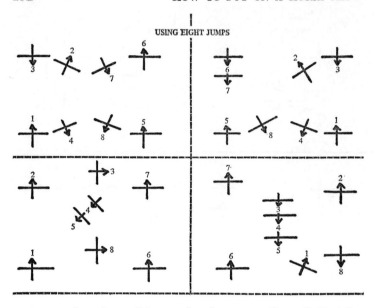

same number, but add a. or b. after it, as 7a and 7b. This will tell both the contestants and the judge that this is a combination. In counting the number of jumps in a course, each jump of a combination is counted separately.

In designing hunter courses where all the action takes place within an arena, one tries to lay out a course where the pace, manner of going, jumping style, and way of covering the course can be readily seen by the judge. Thus, one tries to lay out the course so that there is at least one change of lead required, and the contestant has to travel a full length of the arena without any jump to interfere with his pace and way of going.

Again, in choosing the jumps to use, the designer selects representatives of those that would actually be found in a real hunt. This bars the use of such jumps as triple bars and hogbacks. He will use banks if available, and water jumps, in addition to the usual stone walls, fences, gates, coops, and natural rails.

The average height for most jumps on a hunter course is four feet, although they may go as high as four feet, six inches. There is no need to raise any of the fences after a round, since there is no jump-off as there is in jumper classes. In handy hunter classes, the agility of the horse is a prime factor, hence the designer puts in quick turns where handiness counts. Height is not as important as the handiness of the course.

As said before, not all jumpers are hunters, but all hunters are expected to jump. But his jumping must be smooth, bold, and even. The courses should be laid out to allow the good hunter to show himself at his best.

APPENDIX H
JUMP CONSTRUCTION

There are many types of jumps: brush, fences, banks, water, post and rails, walls, coops, etc. These can be placed into two categories: those movable and those fixed. The movable ones are the kind one sees at most horse shows. The fixed ones are found mostly on cross-country courses, or courses outside of the show ring.

On the next few pages plans and drawings for making certain movable jumps are shown. These are rather common and are of the kind most found in show jumping. There are many others that can be designed by an experienced person, usually an adaptation of some jump he has seen previously. By using the jumps shown here, along with the use of potted plants obtained from a local

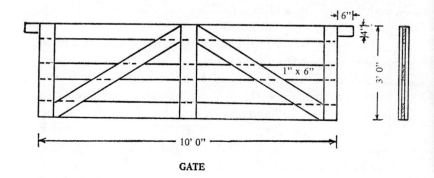

6"

4"

3' 0"

1" x 6"

10' 0"

GATE

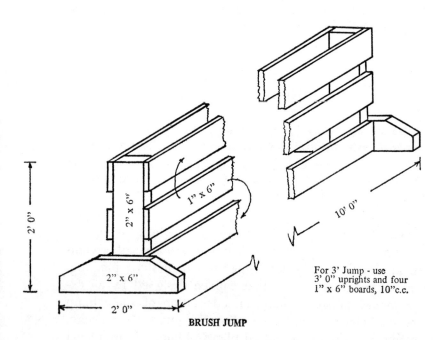

2' 0"

2" x 6"

1" x 6"

2" x 6"

2' 0"

10' 0"

For 3' Jump - use
3' 0" uprights and four
1" x 6" boards, 10"c.c.

BRUSH JUMP

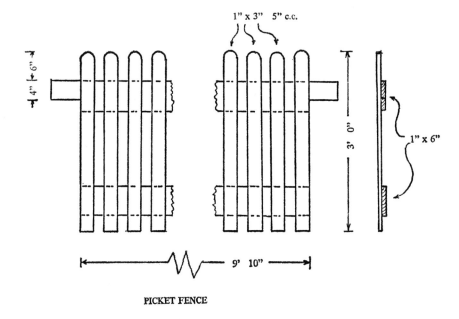

1" x 3"   5" c.c.

4"   6"

3' 0"

1" x 6"

9'   10"

PICKET FENCE

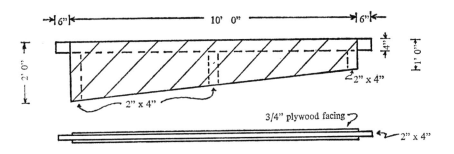

6"   10' 0"   6"

2' 0"

4"

1' 0"

2" x 4"

2" x 4"

3/4" plywood facing

2" x 4"

R.R.   X–ING

Paint 1'-0" Black and Yellow Stripes
diagonally on both faces

nursery, a few bales of hay, and some cut brush to be laid on the ground, quite a few good courses may be set up.

In making jumps, top grade lumber should be used, especially in constructing poles. It should be dry, with good grain, and painted when finished. White is the simplest color to use, but colors and combinations thereof make for eye-pleasing arenas. Red and white, blue and white, green and white, red and yellow, and any combination of the basic colors can be used.

Nails are the most common means of fastening the jumps together, but bolts and screws should be used in making the bases. At a show, it is a must to have a can of assorted nails, a hammer, and a small saw handy to make rapid repairs when a jump is damaged. A few pieces of 1" x 2" lumber can be useful also.

The heights shown on the posts will suffice for most affairs. However, if the type of competition warrants higher posts, they must either be made taller, or blocks be put under them so as to raise them. For this purpose, one should have on hand about six to eight blocks, 6" x 6", 30" long. These can also be used under the brush jumps, stone wall, triple bar, and wherever needed.

A vertical jump is one in which all elements are in the same vertical plane. A spread jump is one in which the elements of the jump are in different planes. The spread of a jump is measured between the two outermost extremities in a horizontal line. A wall or a coop is a spread jump, while a post and rail by itself is a vertical jump. Spread jumps may be made by using a brush and a post and rail, or two posts and rails, or other combinations, remembering that the furthest element should not be lower than any previous element.

CHICKEN COOP

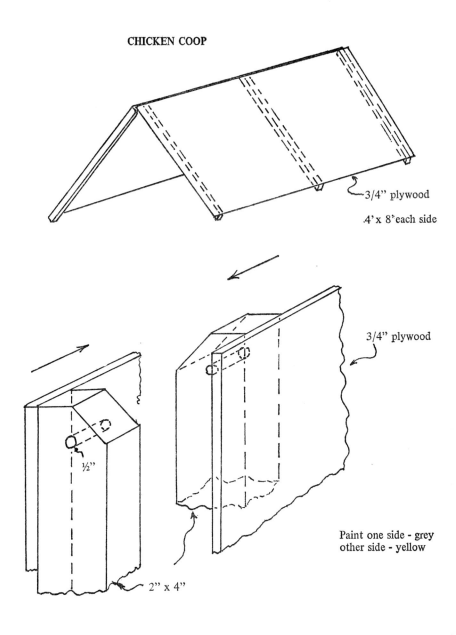

3/4" plywood

4' x 8' each side

3/4" plywood

½"

2" x 4"

Paint one side - grey
other side - yellow

HINGE DETAIL

Use 7/16" bolt in 1/2" holes

Height of jump is controlled by spread

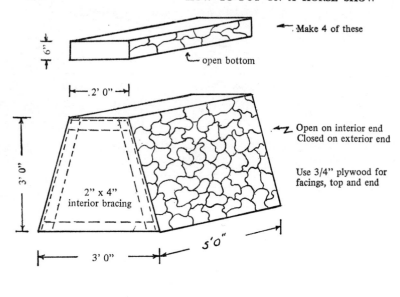

6"

Make 4 of these

open bottom

2' 0"

3' 0"

2" x 4"
interior bracing

Open on interior end
Closed on exterior end

Use 3/4" plywood for
facings, top and end

3' 0"

5'0"

STONE WALL   *(one half shown)*

Make other half to fit together for 10' 0" width
Paint both faces grey with 1/2" black lines to
simulate rock wall
By using 6" x 2' 0" x 5' 0" boxes, height may be raised to 4' 0"

With the exception of the triple bar, all the jumps illustrated can be used in hunter courses. These are the type of jumps usually found in the hunting field. Rails must not be used on top of the brush jumps in hunter courses. The jumps will represent the hedges found in the field, which have no rails above them.

If natural poles can be found, these make excellent substitutes for the man-made rails in hunter classes. They add color and naturalness to such courses. Care must be taken in the selection of natural rails so that they are chosen from wood that will not split easily.

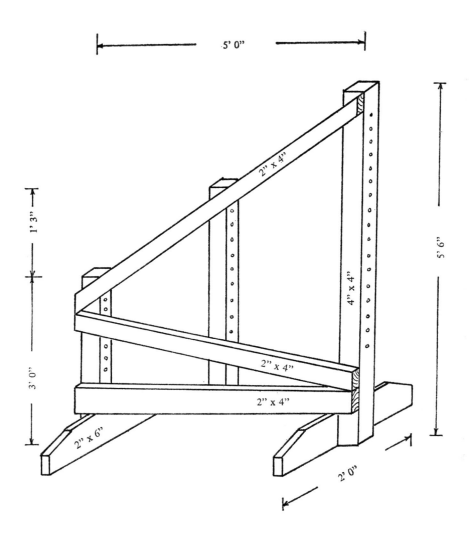

STANDARD FOR TRIPLE BAR JUMP

Right side shown
Make left side to complement

Drill ½" holes — same spacing as
on posts for post and rails

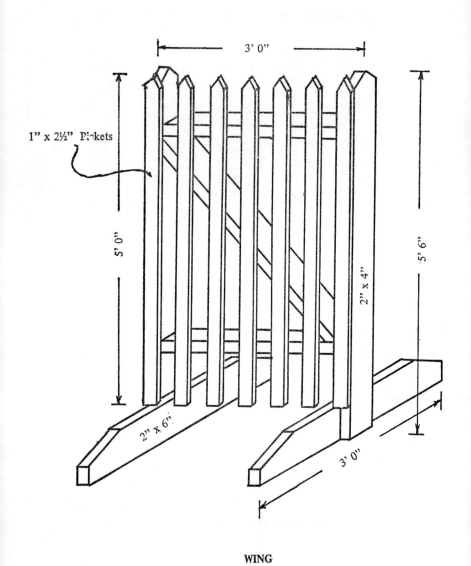

3' 0"

1" x 2½" Pickets

5' 0"

5' 6"

2" x 4"

2" x 6"

3' 0"

WING

COMBINATION WING & POST

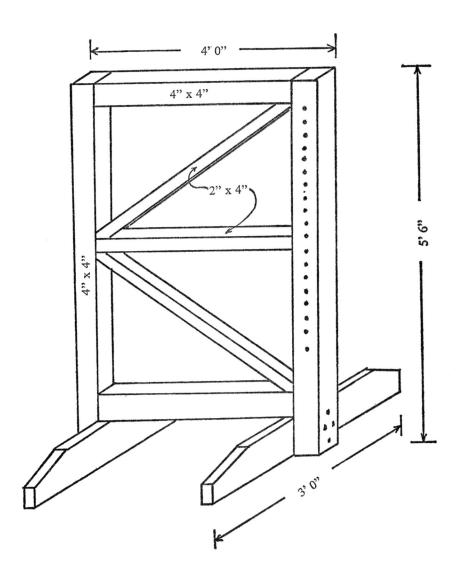

POST FOR POST & RAILS

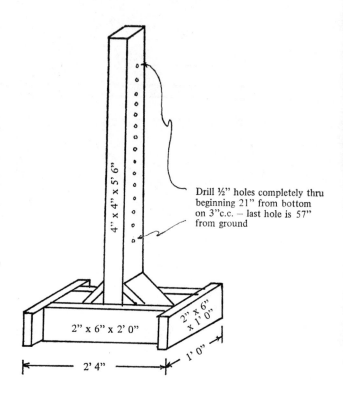

4" x 4" x 5' 6"

Drill ½" holes completely thru
beginning 21" from bottom
on 3"c.c. — last hole is 57"
from ground

2" x 6" x 2' 0"

2" x 6" x 1' 0"

1' 0"

2' 4"

For rails — Trim 4" x 4" x 12' 0" as shown

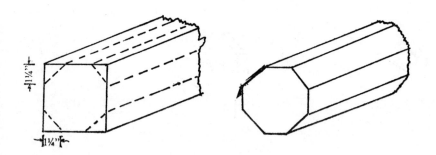

1¼"

1¼"

Hanger Cups

On the opposite page is shown a pattern and plan for hanger cups to be used on posts, as rests for the poles. They may also be used as rests for the railroad crossing, picket fence, or gate.

Cut 5″ x 12″ flat ⅛″ sheet iron.

Cut from A to B to C (Figure 1).

Cut from D to E to F (Figure 1).

Cut ½″ holes where indicated.

Fold small piece out at 90 degrees along C-D.

Fold large piece back at 90 degrees along H-G and I-K.

Curve small piece as in BCDE (Figure 2).

Weld small piece to face of large piece along M-C and D-N (Figure 2).

When finished, it is a slip-on sleeve with 5″ x 1½″ cup. It fits on the post and is held in place by a ⅜″ bolt, 5″ in length. Different heights may be obtained by moving sleeve up or down the post. It is a good practice to have a few more bolts than cups on hand as they can become lost in the footing when the jumps are being shifted around.

There are several types of cups available commercially, and many others that have been designed and are in use. The key in design is to be sure the cup is the regulation size, as required by the rules of the American Horse Shows Association, and to have it easily movable up or down along the post.

APPENDIX I
OUTSIDE COURSES

Outside courses and cross-country courses are used in hunter classes and as part of a combined training event.

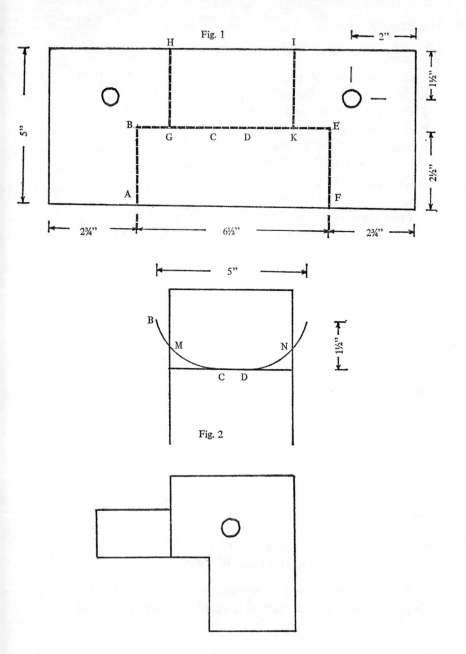

Fig. 1

Fig. 2

In designing such courses one should use the natural lay of the land as much as possible. Most of the jumps on either type will be permanent and fixed in position.

In an outside hunter course, the length may run from about 400 to 1000 yards. These are located in the vicinity of the main arena, and the course may come in and out of the arena. All the jumps on the course should be visible to the judge, since these and hunters and being looked at accordingly.

For cross-country courses, it is a different matter. This part of a combined training affair is considered to be the most difficult. Therefore the course will be anywhere from two to five miles or more in length, and will have from 15 to 25 jumps or obstacles. Courses for training divisions may be shorter but seldom less than a mile and a half.

The following examples are from the booklet, *Notes on Dressage and Combined Training,* published by the American Horse Shows Association in collaboration with the United States Combined Training Association and the United States Pony Clubs, Inc. They are furnished through the courtesy of the American Horse Shows Association. Note that the profile illustrations represent a few types of obstacles suitable for *Moderate* open competitions.

APPENDIX J
TRAIL HORSE CLASSES

The next few pages on Trail Horse Classes are courtesy of the Pacific Coast Hunter, Jumper and Stock Horse Association, and are from its 1969 rule book. It is intended to help the management in setting up trail courses.

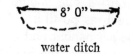

water ditch

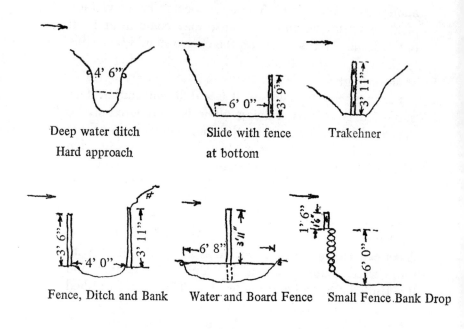

Deep water ditch
Hard approach

Slide with fence
at bottom

Trakehner

Fence, Ditch and Bank

Water and Board Fence

Small Fence Bank Drop

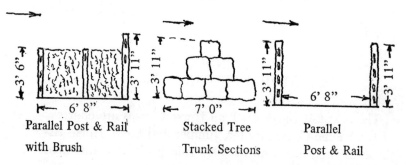

Parallel Post & Rail
with Brush

Stacked Tree
Trunk Sections

Parallel
Post & Rail

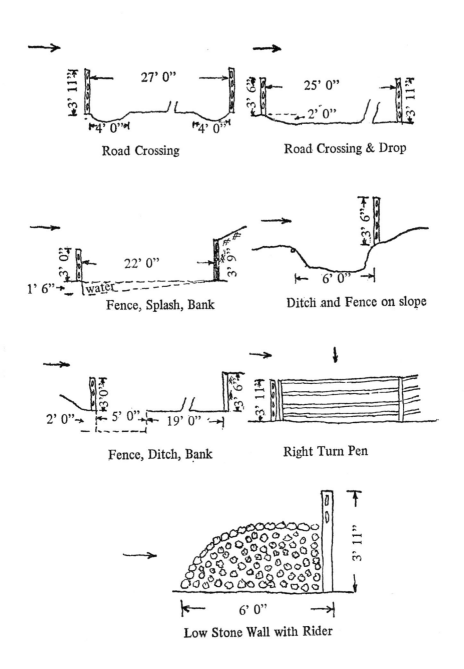

Road Crossing

Road Crossing & Drop

Fence, Splash, Bank

Ditch and Fence on slope

Fence, Ditch, Bank

Right Turn Pen

Low Stone Wall with Rider

Just as in designing hunter and jumper courses, it is the caliber of the expected competition that determines the degree of difficulty sought.

The PCHJ and SHA recommends that at least six obstacles be used. Even in the smallest shows, there should be at least five. But remember when laying out the course, each go is an individual effort and will take time. Any course taking more than three minutes to get over will consume much time if the class is large. Setting obstacles closer together and jogging between obstacles can speed up the proceedings.

An example of a simple trail course is shown. Even if the courses are posted or sent to the exhibitors ahead of the show, it is still customary to review the course with the judge present so there will be no doubt as to what is intended.

TRAIL HORSE CLASSES

The following material is presented as a guide to horse show managements and committees to help them with the preparation for Trail Horse Classes.

It should be pointed out this Association feels that Trail Horse obstacles and courses should be chosen in such a way as to demonstrate the control, flexibility and calmness of the ideal Trail Horse.

"Horror" courses and impossible obstacles are apparently of no benefit, sometimes resulting in injury to horses and riders and actually increases the burden on those who must judge. All courses are subject to the approval of the judge and the judge has the authority to eliminate any obstacle which he feels is dangerous to horse or rider.

No course may be used twice except in divisional classes (i.e. lightweight, heavyweight; stallions/geldings, mares) which MUST be identical. It is suggested that there be a minimum of six obstacles in any Trail Horse class.

Management MUST give particular thought to the difficulty of the courses as related to the type of class called for. It is obvious that the Trail Stake should be more difficult than the Amateur or Ladies class.

The following classes are listed in order of difficulty and complexity starting with the most simple:

1. Children (12 years and under)
   a. Younger children must not be asked to dismount and/or lead over a jump.
   b. Younger children must not be asked to drag or carry.
2. Children (13 years through 17 years)
3. Ladies and/or Amateur
4. Divisional classes (i.e. lightweight, heavyweight; stallions/geldings, mares)
5. Stake

A show may offer a "horror" or unusual course in addition to the regular point classes. No points will be given. This class must be so described in the prize list and it must be stated that no points will be given.

1. Gates

Gates should be constructed with a minimum of 50 inches from top of gate to ground and a minimum width of 4 feet. Any material is satisfactory, but pipe, as illustrated, is long lasting and will not tip or sag due to cross brace at bottom.

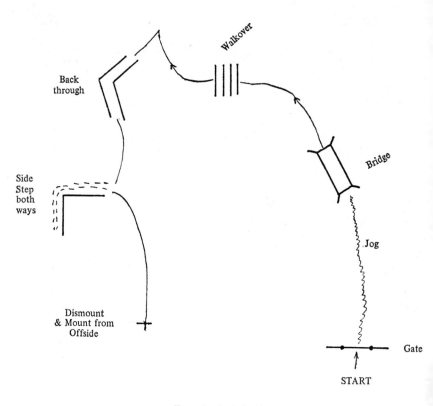

Walkover

Back
through

Bridge

Side
Step
both
ways

Jog

Dismount
& Mount from
Offside

Gate

START

Example of a trail class course

2. Walk Over

May be constructed from a wide variety of objects.
Recommendations:

Single walk-over poles, not to exceed 16" in height.

Multiple poles, not to exceed 10" in height.

In multiple combinations, rolling poles should not be
used.

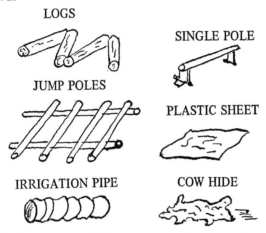

LOGS

SINGLE POLE

JUMP POLES

PLASTIC SHEET

IRRIGATION PIPE   COW HIDE

Hay bales are unsatisfactory as walkovers, due to danger of catching a shoe in wire.

Hides should not be used on bridges or any closer
than 6' to such an element.

3. Walk Through

Water pits, etc., should enable a horse to go through
without injury. Placement of boulders and other hidden
objects beneath the surface is not desirable.

4. Back Through

Recommended:

Minimum width between elements to be 30 inches.

JUMP POLES

WATER HOLE

WATER BOX

TIRES

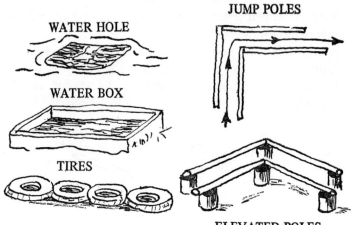

ELEVATED POLES

OIL DRUMS

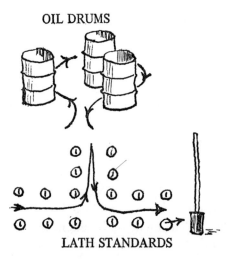

LATH STANDARDS

36 inches is a good average width. Hay bales not desirable due to danger of catching a shoe in the wire. Hay bales are not to be used.

5. Jumps

Jumps may be taken singularly or in combinations. They may also be negotiated mounted or with the rider dismounted and leading his horse across.

Recommended: Mounted—maximum height 24 inches
Lead over—maximum height 18 inches
In all cases at least 4 feet wide.

JUMP POLES    LOG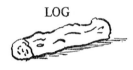

6. Bridge

Bridges should be of sturdy construction with a minimum width of 36 inches and with non-slip ramp approaches.

7. Side Passes

This exercise may be conducted over a single pole, between parallel poles or around corners, either straddling a pole or between poles.

Hay bales are again not desirable for this maneuver due to danger of catching a shoe in the wire. Hay bales are not to be used.

8. Dismounted Maneuvers *

These are varied and may include:

1. Leading over jumps

* Note to Management: It has been found, particularly in classes with large numbers of entries, that dismounted maneuvers are extremely time consuming and often triple in the length of time necessary to get a horse over the course. In childrens' classes they even waste more time due to the difficulty of dismounting and mounting.

2. Loading into horse trailer
3. Hobbling or ground tying

9. *Rail Work*

Horses are to be shown at the walk, jog and lope both directions of the ring. A minimum of once around the ring at the jog and lope is suggested, however excessive rail work is to be discouraged.

APPENDIX K
DRESSAGE COMPETITIONS

Dressage competitions require an arena of specific dimensions. There are two sizes, as shown in the following illustration. The size used will depend on the level of competition.

The arena should be level and the footing should be grass, sand, dirt, or a mixture. It should be solid under the horse and not too deep. The arena should be enclosed with a low fence, not over 16 inches in height. At A in the drawing there should be an easily movable section of fence to allow easy entry for the exhibitor.

An example of a dressage ride score sheet is given. These vary for different levels and are changed from time to time. The current tests for each level may be obtained from the American Horse Shows Association. For combined training events, it is best to obtain them from the United States Combined Training Association, whose address appears in Appendix N in this book.

Again, it is recommended that before considering a dressage event, it is well to study the pamphlet, *Notes on Dressage and Combined Training,* published by AHSA.

ARENAS FOR DRESSAGE COMPETITIONS

1 meter = 3.3 feet

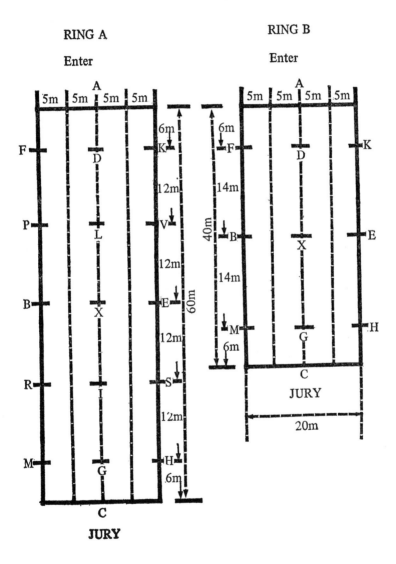

RING A

Enter

RING B

Enter

AMERICAN HORSE SHOWS ASSOCIATION

First Level Dressage Test 1

PURPOSE: To determine that the correct foundation has been laid for successful further training, i.e., that the horse moves freely forward in a relaxed manner and with rhythm, accepts the bit and is obedient to the rider's aids.

CONDITIONS: a) To be ridden in a plain snaffle with or without dropped noseband.
b) Arena size: 20 m. x 40 m. (66' x 132').

SCORING:

10 Excellent	6 Satisfactory	2 Bad
9 Very Good	5 Sufficient	1 Very Bad
8 Good	4 Insufficient	0 Not Performed
7 Fairly Good	3 Fairly Bad	

PENALTIES: Time: 1 point for each commenced 5 seconds overtime.

Errors: 1st error, 2 points; 2nd error, 5 points; 3rd error, elimination; leaving arena, elimination. (When test is part of a combined event, 3rd error is penalized with 10 points and 4th error causes elimination.)

CONTESTANT'S NUMBER_____
RIDER _____
HORSE _____

		TEST	POINTS	REMARKS
1	A	Enter ordinary walk.		
	X	Halt. Salute. Proceed ordinary trot (sitting).		
	C	Track to the right.		
2	M-X-K	Change rein, ordinary trot (rising).		
	K	Ordinary trot (sitting).		
3	F-X-H	Change rein, ordinary trot (rising).		
	H	Ordinary trot (sitting).		
4	B	Ordinary walk.		
	A	Halt. Half turn on forehand left. Proceed ordinary walk.		
5	B	Halt. Half turn on forehand right. Proceed at ordinary walk.		

6	F	Ordinary trot (sitting).		
	A	Canter, right lead, and circle 20 m. (66') diameter, once around.		
7	K-X-M	Change rein.		
	M	Change lead by passing for 2 or 3 strides through the trot.		
8	C	Circle, 20 m. (66') diameter, once around.		
9	H-X-F	Change rein.		
	F	Change lead by passing for 2 or 3 strides through the trot.		
10	H	Ordinary trot (sitting).		
	C-A	Serpentine of 3 loops—width of arena (5 loops in large arena).		
	A	Track to the right.		
11	K-X-M	Change rein, strong trot (rising).		
	M	Ordinary trot (sitting).		
12	H-X-F	Change rein, strong trot (sitting).		
	F	Ordinary trot (sitting).		
13	K-X-M	Change rein.		
	X	Halt. Immobile 5 seconds. Proceed ordinary trot (sitting).		
14	C	Ordinary walk.		
	H-X-F	Change rein, free walk.		
	F	Ordinary walk.		
15	A	Down center line, ordinary trot (sitting).		
	G	Halt. Salute. Leave arena free walk.		
16*		Jump one fence about 75cm. (2'6"). (Two efforts allowed.) Scored on willingness of horse and general obedience only.		
		GENERAL IMPRESSIONS		
17		Paces (regularity and freedom).		
18		Impulsion.		
19		Obedience, lightness and suppleness of horse.		
20		Position and seat of rider. Correct use of aids.		

* *Note:* Jumping is not required when the test is part of a combined event.

Point To Be Deducted: Total Points _____

                                    Time _____

                                    Error _____

                                    Final Score _____

1/1/65   Judge's Signature _____

APPENDIX L
COMPETITIVE TRAIL RIDES

On the following pages are shown an information sheet and an entry form for a competitive trail ride. The information sheet corresponds to the prize list for a horse show. It gives just about all the information that a prospective contestant needs to know in order to enter.

The first and second sheets were printed back to back, the entry form inserted, and then the whole thing folded twice and stapled. This made a mailing piece of about 4½″ by 7″. The original size of each sheet was legal size, 8½″ by 14.″ There was some extra space available for advertising, which helped defray the cost of printing.

Since competitive trail rides are held over quite a distance, the starting point, or base, may not be known to everyone. Therefore directions about how to get there should be specific. More than once competitors have arrived quite late, after wandering around the country for several hours trying to find the place. Markers and directional signs the last few miles along the way are quite helpful.

ENTRY BLANK AND MEAL RESERVATIONS

Annual Spring Trail Ride

CONCORD MT. DIABLO TRAIL RIDE ASSOCIATION, INC.
CLAYTON, CALIFORNIA

APRIL 17, 18, 19, 1970

USE SEPARATE ENTRY FOR EACH PERSON

Deadline for Entries
and Reservations
APRIL 15, 1970

THE RIDE WILL BE LIMITED TO 100 ENTRIES. MAIL YOUR ENTRY EARLY!

THE POSTMARK DATE WILL BE THE DETERMING FACTORS

Name of Person (print) _____
                                    (FIRST)   (LAST)

Address _____ Phone _____

DIVISION ENTERED:

☐ Heavyweight (190 # & over)   ☐ Lightweight (155 #—189 #)   ☐ Junior (Age 10-17)
☐ Novice Senior   ☐ Novice Junior   ☐ Non-rider

Birthdate of Junior: _____

CSHA Annual Award for Juniors and Seniors . . . Are you a member of CSHA?
Club Affiliated................   Individual Member ....

NAME OF HORSE	BREED	REG. #	COLOR	SEX	WGT.	AGE

Owner of Horse: _____

Computation of Fees:	Entry Fees	Indicate your Reservations below	FOR NON-RIDERS:	Meal Reservations	Indicate your Reservations below
Lightweight			Friday Dinner	$1.85	
or Heavyweight	$24.00		Saturday Breakfast	1.85	
Junior NATRC	23.00		Saturday Lunch	1.50	
Novice Senior	24.00		Saturday Dinner	2.75	
Novice Junior	23.00		Sunday Breakfast	1.85	
			Sunday Lunch	1.50	

TOTAL for MEALS: $ _____   TOTAL AMOUNT $ _____

NOTE: ALL MEALS FOR COMPETING RIDERS ARE INCLUDED IN ENTRY FEE.

I hereby release the Concord-Mt. Diablo Trail Ride Association, Inc. and the officers and members thereof, and each of them from all and every claim for damages which may occur to me, my horse, or property, at any time hereafter, in favor of myself, my heirs, representatives or dependents, against said Concord-Mt. Diablo Trail Ride Association, Inc., its officers, members, or any of them, by reason of any injuries, loss or damages, which may be suffered by me, or them, or any of them because of any matter, thing or condition, negligence, or default whatsoever, and I hereby assume and accept the full risk and danger of any hurt, injury or damage which may occur through or by reason of, any matter, thing, condition, negligence or default, or any person or persons whatsoever, in any of the activities held, or given, by or under the direction of said Concord Mt. Diablo Trail Ride Association, Inc.

I hereby consent to the entry of my child in the Mt. Diablo Ride

Signature of Exhibitor _____   Signature of Parent or Guardian of Minor _____

Exhibitor's Name: _____   Address _____
City and State _____   Phone _____
No Entries accepted unless this form is signed.   All Entry Fees must accompany Entry.

Please mail all Entries and Reservations to . . .
FRED KIRKHAM, Ride Chairman . . . P. O. Box 4068, Walnut Creek, California 94596

Checks should be payable to: CONCORD—MT. DIABLO TRAIL RIDE ASSOC., INC.
For additional information . . . phone: 935-1990 — 934-0222 — 885-5403 — 686-1156 —
685-6114 — 452-1552

FELLOW HORSEMEN:

THE ANNUAL CONCORD-MT. DIABLO SPRING TRAIL RIDE will be held on SATURDAY—APRIL 18, 1970; It will be sanctioned by the North American Trail Ride Conference and conducted under the rules as published in the NATRC Rule Book, 1970 Edition. Class B Points will be awarded in accordance with the revised point schedule.

The ride will start from the Club Grounds located 2½ miles east of Clayton, off Marsh Creek Road. Clayton may be reached by proceeding east on Clayton Rd. from Concord, California. Once past Clayton, proceed east on Marsh Creek Road until the sign "Russelman Park" is reached, turn south up the mountain approximately 1 mile to the Club Grounds.

Starting time is 7:30 a.m. Saturday morning and final judging will take place Sunday morning. Horses should be checked in as early as possible Friday afternoon, April 17, 1970.

The Novice Division is open to any rider, 10 years of age or older, never having won a national championship or placed third or higher in NATRC annual high scores in any division in any previous year. Horses over 5 years of age may compete in the Novice Division until they have accumulated 32 points. Thereafter, they must enter other divisions. Horses less than 5 years of age must compete in this division. Horses less than 36 months old will not be allowed to compete. Annual high score awards and national championships will not be awarded nor will rider be eligible for annual horsemanship awards in this division. The ride will be over a shortened course and will be divided into Junior and Senior sections.

Thus, the ride will be divided into five divisions:

HEAVYWEIGHT (190 pounds or over, rider, equipment and tack); LIGHTWEIGHT (155 pounds minimum to 189 pounds maximum); JUNIOR (10 years through 17 years of age—no weight limit); NOVICE SENIOR, (18 years of age or more); NOVICE JUNIOR (10 through 17 years of age).

Horses are to be shod with metal shoes and are subject to farrier examination. Use of boots, pads, wraps, bandages, medicine, ice, stimulants or ice water is not permitted. Medication, however, under the supervision, direction and approval of the ride veterinarian and upon his prescription is permissible. Juniors will not be permitted to ride stallions. A saddle must be used, but type as well as all other tack is optional. Participants should bring their own sleeping gear, horse equipment, grooming equipment, hay, as well as any grain desired. Riders who abuse their horses will be disqualified and asked to leave.

Trophies will be awarded for first place in each division as well as a sweepstakes trophy for the Heavyweight, Lightweight and Junior Divisions. Ribbons will be awarded through sixth place. Horsemanship trophies for first place in Senior and Junior Divisions with ribbons through sixth place to be awarded. Inasmuch as the ride has been registered with the California State Horsemen's Association, placement in the Junior Division and/or the Junior Horsemanship Division will earn credits for the CSHA Junior High Point Program.

Entry fees for Heavyweight, Lightweight and Novice Senior riders will be $24.00, and for Juniors and Novice Junior Riders $23.00. These fees will include Friday dinner; Saturday breakfast, lunch and dinner; Sunday breakfast and lunch. It also includes NATRC Fees, use of tie stalls, bedding for horses, and a $1.00 refundable deposit for the riders number.

APPENDIX M
AHSA AFFILIATED ASSOCIATIONS

This list of associations appearing below is furnished from the 1969 rule book of the American Horse Shows Association, through the courtesy of that organization.

Some of these sponsor shows and some sponsor competitions with awards to the high point horses or contestants in different categories. Before considering asking a sanction from any of these, it is best to write for information.

These are all associations affiliated with the AHSA. Such associations are groups of shows in a state or locality, or other organizations, approved by the AHSA Executive Committee, which have joined together to form an association.

The Association welcomes the organizations listed below as 1969 Affiliated Association Members. These associations have by their affiliation indicated their belief in the principles for which we stand. However, shows belonging to an Affiliated Association are not permitted to advertise themselves as recognized shows.

AMERICAN HACKNEY HORSE SOCIETY
    Pres.—Mrs. Alan R. Robson, R.D. 3, West Chester, Pa.
    Sec.—Miss Susan Saltonstall, Lone Oak Fm., Dover, Mass.
    Corres. to: 527 Madison Avenue, New York, N. Y. 10022
AMERICAN SADDLEBRED PLEASURE HORSE ASSN.
    Pres.—Robert Leu, Main St. Rd., Keokuk, Iowa 52632

Sec.—Miss Irene Zane, 801 S. Court St., Scott City, Kan.

AMERICAN SADDLE HORSE BREEDERS ASSN.

Pres.—T. J. Morton, Jr., Old Stone House, Newburgh, Ind.

Sec.—C. J. Cronan, Jr., 929 S. Fourth St., Louisville, Ky.

AMERICAN SHETLAND PONY CLUB

Pres.—T. R. Huston, Box 236, Hanna City, Ill.

Sec.—Burton J. Zuege, P.O. Box 2339, W. Lafayette, Ind.

AMERICAN WALKING HORSE ASSN.

Pres.—Cebern Lee, Leeswood, Oaks Corners, N. Y. 14518

Sec.—Mrs. P. R. Marble, 753 Herkimer Rd., Utica, N. Y. 13502

ARIZONA HORSE EXHIBITORS ASSN.

Pres.—G. P. Lasley, 5632 E. Calle Camelia, Phoenix, Ariz.

Sec.—Ruth Adams, 1805 E. Myrtle Ave., Phoenix, Ariz.

ARIZONA PROFESSIONAL HORSEMEN'S ASSN.

Pres.—Dwight D. Stewart, R.F.D. 1, Box 782, Prescott, Ariz.

Sec.—Miss Pat O'Leary, 7824 N. 15th Ave., Phoenix, Ariz.

CALIFORNIA PROFESSIONAL HORSEMEN'S ASSN.

Pres.—Sandy Sanders, P.O. Box 296, Goleta, Calif. 93107

Sec.—Glen Gimple, 1405 Encino, Monrovia, Calif. 91016

CALIFORNIA STATE HORSEMEN'S ASSN.

Pres.—Geo. M. Dean, 540 Laurent Rd., Hillsborough, Cal.

Sec.—Mrs. Betty Menefee, P.O. Box 1179, Santa Rosa, Cal.

CENTRAL OHIO SADDLE CLUB

Pres.—John Liston, 380 Robertsville Ave., S.E., Minerva, Ohio

Sec.–Norma Miller, 6824 Whipple Ave., N.W., N. Canton, Ohio

CONNECTICUT HORSE SHOWS ASSN.

Pres.–R. M. Welton, Roast Meat Hill Rd., Killingworth, Conn.

Sec.–Mrs. D. W. Cornwell, 609 Highland St., Weathersfield, Conn.

CONNECTICUT HUNTER-JUMPER ASSN.

Pres.–Carey Williams, Box 89, Woodstock, Conn. 06281

Sec.–Mrs. W. G. Buckley, Pond Meadow Rd., Westbrook, Conn.

EASTERN SADDLE HORSE BREEDERS ASSN.

Pres.–J. Wingate Brown, 169 E. 78th St., New York, N. Y.

Sec.–Mrs. R. F. Jones, 116 Washington St., E. Stroudsburg, Pa.

EMPIRE STATE HORSEMEN'S ASSN.

Pres.–Joseph A. Vanorio, Box 142B, Pound Ridge, N. Y.

Sec.–Mrs. R. F. Rodricks, 875 King St., Chappaqua, N. Y.

Corres. to: P.O. Box 41, Pound Ridge, N. Y. 10576

EQUESTRIAN TRAILS, INC.

Pres.–Frank Hall, 10639 Riverside Dr., N. Hollywood, Cal.

Sec.–Sharon Chivell, 10639 Riverside Dr., N. Hollywood, Cal.

Corres. to: Kay Devin, 10639 Riverside Dr., N. Hollywood, Cal.

FLORIDA HUNTER AND JUMPER ASSN.

Pres.–Mrs. M. R. Harden, 7400 S.W. 68th Ct., S. Miami, Fla.

Sec.–Miss Sandy Shultz, 398 Ocean Dr., Boca Raton, Fla.

HAWAII HORSE SHOW ASSN.
Pres.—Mrs. H. B. Clark, Jr., 3060 Noela Dr., Honolulu, Hawaii
Sec.—Mrs. Chas. Pietsch, 4330 PuuPanini Ave., Honolulu, Hawaii

HUNTER-JUMPER ASSOCIATION OF ALABAMA
Pres.—Dr. J. M. Barnes, 311 So. Perry St., Montgomery, Ala.
Sec.—Mrs. M. G. Hoyle, Rt. 4, Box 341, Montgomery, Ala.

ILLINOIS HORSE OF THE YEAR ASSN.
Pres.—Wm. C. Wright, Box 8126, Milwaukee, Wis.
Sec.—Florence M. Mueller, 625 Arlington Pl., Chicago, Ill.

INTER-COUNTY HORSEMEN'S ASSN.
Pres.—Ray First, R.D. 1, Fredonia, Pa.
Sec.—Mrs. Edward Ulp, Box 111, Brookfield, Ohio 44403

INTERNATIONAL ARABIAN HORSE ASSN.
Pres.—Jay W. Stream, Rt. 3, Box 212, San Luis Obispo, Cal.
Sec.—Mrs. Edith Rosenberg, No. Main St., Abbeville, S. C.
Corres. to: R. E. Goodall, 224 E. Olive Ave., Burbank, Cal.

INTER-STATE HORSE SHOW ASSN.
Pres.—J. C. Solomon, 229 Pleasant St., Morgantown, W. Va.
Sec.—Mrs. A. M. Souders, R.D. 3, Morningside, Waynesburg, Pa.

KANSAS SADDLE HORSE ASSN.
Pres.—James A. Wilson, R.R. 2, Olathe, Kan. 66061

Sec.–Mr. Cleo Ray, 807 N. Topeka, Wichita, Kan. 67214

KENTUCKY ASSN. OF FAIRS & HORSE SHOWS

Pres.–C. M. Shewmaker, 540 N. College St., Harrodsburg, Ky.

Sec.–W. M. Mumford, Jr., P.O. Box 188, Campbellsville, Ky.

KENTUCKY HUNTER & JUMPER ASSN.

Pres.–Mrs. T. O. Campbell, Winchester Rd., Lexington, Ky.

Sec.–Mrs. Robt. Murphy, Rt. 7, Grimes Mill Rd., Lexington, Ky.

LOS ANGELES CO. HORSE SHOW EXHIBITORS ASSN.

Pres.–Bob Jones, 17809 Kinzie St., Northridge, Cal.

Sec.–Susan Sullivan, 17809 Kinzie St., Northridge, Cal.

MAINE HORSE ASSN.

Pres.–Joseph Palleschi, R.F.D. 3, Winthrop, Me.

Sec.–Sandie Crossley, R. 1, Box 240, Greene, Maine

MARYLAND HORSE SHOWS ASSN.

Pres.–Thomas W. Hoffecker, Monkton, Md.

Sec.–John A. Wagner, Jr., Roxhill Farm, Monkton, Md.

MASSACHUSETTS HORSEMEN'S COUNCIL

Pres.–Mrs. Cora Snow, 495 Pearl St., Brockton, Mass.

Sec.–Mrs. L. C. Bird, Box 117, Grove St., Upton, Mass.

MICHIGAN HORSE SHOWS ASSN.

Pres.–Norman J. Ellis, 7425 Lahser Rd., Birmingham, Mich.

Sec.–Mrs. H. E. Pedersen, 381 Golfcrest Dr., Dearborn, Mich.

MID-SOUTH HORSE SHOWS ASSN.

Pres.–Robert Henson, Box 1806, Jackson, Tenn.

Sec.–Emmet Guy, Box 1806, Jackson, Tenn.

MISSOURI HORSE SHOWS ASSN.
Pres.—D. K. Gash, 91st & Raytown Rd., Kansas City, Mo.
Sec.—Mrs. Martha Thompson, Rt. 6, Columbia, Mo.

MORGAN HORSE CLUB
Pres.—Deane C. Davis, Dyer Ave., Montpelier, Vt.
Sec.—Seth P. Holcombe, Box 2157, W. Hartford, Conn.

NATIONAL HALF-WALKER BREEDERS ASSN.
Pres.—H. D. Thompson, Box 442, Mansfield, Ohio
Sec.—Mrs. Helene Thompson, Box 442, Mansfield, Ohio

NEVADA SADDLE, HUNT & HARNESS ASSN.
Pres.—Les Keller, Rt. 1, Box 13, Yerington, Nev.
Sec.—Wendy VonFluee, 905 Juniper Hill Rd., Reno, Nev.

NEVADA STATE HORSEMEN'S ASSN.
Pres.—Penny Whalen, 1105 Sbragia Way, Sparks, Nev.
Sec.—Mrs. Barbara Fullman, 1738 Cristy La., Las Vegas, Nev.

NEW ENGLAND HORSEMEN'S COUNCIL
Pres.—Mrs. M. LeBoff, 20 Dover Rd., Newington, Conn.
Sec.—A. F. Denghausen, 6 Abby Ave., Warwick, R. I.

NEW HAMPSHIRE HORSE & TRAIL ASSN.
Pres.—Lester Spear, Appleton St., E. Concord, N. H.
Sec.—Florence William, R.D. 2, Box 132, Manchester, N. H.
Corres. to: Mrs. N. F. Bigelow, 11 Shirley Pk., Goffstown, N. H.

OREGON HORSEMEN'S ASSN.
Pres.—Dr. Harold E. Davis, Wilsonville, Ore.
Sec.—Mrs. Linda McKay, Rt. 1, Box 15, Eagle Creek, Ore.

PACIFIC COAST HUNTER, JUMPER & STOCK HORSE

Pres.—O. L. Lott, 158 Verde Mesa, Danville, Cal.

Sec.—Marge Trimble, 3301 Sheldon St., Sacramento, Cal.

PALOMINO HORSE BREEDERS OF AMERICA

Pres.—Jay F. Kratz, 113–115 Main, No. Wales, Pa.

Sec.—Howard Grekel, Rt. 1, Box 540, Claremore, Okla.

Corres. to: M. L. Spivey, Box 249, Mineral Wells, Tex.

PENN-OHIO HORSEMEN'S ASSN.

Pres.—Raymond G. Rowles, 4900 Cooper Rd., Lowellville, Ohio

Sec.—Mary G. Rowles, 4900 Cooper Rd., Lowellville, Ohio

PENNSYLVANIA HORSE BREEDERS ASSN.

Pres.—D. D. Odell, 1106 Three Penn Ctr. Plaza, Phila., Pa.

Sec.—R. I. G. Jones, 1310 King St., Wilmington, Del.

Corres. to: 514 Land Title Bldg., Philadelphia, Pa.

PINTO HORSE ASSN. OF AMERICA

Pres.—Ellen S. Davis, P.O. Box 3984, San Diego, Cal.

Sec.—Helen H. Smith, 8245 Hillside Ave., Alta Loma, Cal.

PONY OF THE AMERICAS CLUB

Pres.—James S. Bicknell, Box 67, Clare, Mich.

Sec.—L. L. Boomhower, 1452 No. Federal, Mason City, Iowa

PROFESSIONAL HORSEMEN'S ASSN. OF AMERICA

Pres.—Joseph Moloney, Swamp Rd., Furlong, Pa.

Sec.—Mrs. Harry Black, Sewickley Hunt, Sewickley, Pa.

RHODE ISLAND HORSEMEN'S ASSN.

Pres.—Warren B. Finn, 530 Main St., E. Greenwich, R. I.

Sec.—Earl C. Whelden, Jr., Box 25, Warwick, R. I.
ROCKY MOUNTAIN HORSE SHOW ASSN.
Pres.—Harold Tousignaut, 5110 S. Franklin, Littleton, Colo.
Sec.—Mrs. C. E. Fox, Qtrs. 4170, U.S.A.F. Academy, Colo.
SOUTH CAROLINA HORSE SHOWS ASSN.
Pres.—W. L. Ashley, Abbeville, S. C.
Sec.—J. M. Green, III, Box 514, Orangeburg, S. C.
TENNESSEE WALKING HORSE BREEDERS ASSN.
Pres.—Sen. J. T. Kelley, Rt. 7, Columbia, Tenn.
Sec.—Mrs. Sharon Brandon, Box 286, Lewisburg, Tenn.
TEXAS HUNTER & JUMPER ASSN.
Pres.—James V. Whaley, P.O. Box 523, Marshall, Tex.
Sec.—Mrs. E. R. Miller, 1632 Norfolk St., Houston, Tex.
TRI-STATE HORSEMEN'S ASSN.
Pres.—E. F. Speltz, Rt. 3, Box 21, Stillwater, Minn.
Sec.—Jean Gilligan, Rt. 1, Box 81A, Delano, Minn.
TRI-STATE HORSE SHOWS ASSN.
Pres.—R. Strasburger, 1834 Carriage Rd., Rt. 1, Powell, Ohio
Sec.—Mrs. D. F. Morris, 5145 Morse Rd., Gahanna, Ohio
UNITED STATES EQUESTRIAN TEAM
Pres.—Whitney Stone, 90 Broad St., New York, N. Y.
Sec.—George Merck, U.S.E.T., Gladstone, N. J.
VERMONT HORSE SHOWS ASSN.
Pres.—J. H. Bushor, 4 Kiniry St., Windsor, Vt.
Sec.—Mrs. J. H. Bushor, 4 Kiniry St., Windsor, Vt.
VIRGINIA HORSE SHOWS ASSN.
Pres.—A. Eugene Cunningham, Box 627, Warrenton, Va.
Sec.—Mrs. A. D. Kennedy, Box 1017, Warrenton, Va.

WASHINGTON STATE HORSEMEN
Pres.—Don McCune, 1130 Washington Bldg., Seattle, Wash.

Sec.—Mrs. Ethel Lewis, 3830 134th N.E., Bellevue, Wash.

WELSH PONY SOCIETY OF AMERICA
Pres.—Mrs. R. S. Pirie, Aquila Farm, Hamilton, Mass.

Sec.—Mrs. L. F. Gehret, 1770 Lancaster Ave., Paoli, Pa.

WESTERN HORSEMEN OF OREGON
Pres.—Chuck Maillard, Rt. 3, Box 672, Albany, Ore.

Sec.—Mrs. Cleo Gast, Box 44, Philomath, Ore.

APPENDIX N
OTHER ASSOCIATIONS

The organizations listed below are not affiliated with the American Horse Shows Association, but do sanction and sponsor certain types of equine competition.

American Quarter Horse Association
P. O. Box 200
Amarillo, Texas 79105

Appaloosa Horse Club
P. O. Box 403
Moscow, Idaho

National Cutting Horse Association
P. O. Box 12155
Fort Worth, Texas 76116

North American Trail Ride Conference
1995 Day Road
Gilroy, California 95020

United States Combined Training Association
P. O. Box 143
Leesburg, Virginia 22075

There are many more associations than those that have been listed. Many of them are chapters of some of those listed, while others are smaller organizations but with similar aims. Again, some are quite local in character, but wield quite an influence in their area. Experience and contact with various exhibitors will bring to light all the local associations that must be considered when thinking of sanctions, licenses, sponsorships, etc.

APPENDIX O
TIMING SCHEDULE PRIOR TO THE SHOW

1 year to 9 months:	Decide on type of show.
	Decide on tentative dates.
	Decide on place.
	Form committee.
	Select manager, secretary, treasurer, headquarters, office and address.
	Get sanctions, approvals, licenses.
	Get judges, stewards, veterinarian, farrier, and announcers.
	Set up program committee.
9 to 6 months:	Solicit class sponsors.
	Firm up dates and location.
	Advance publicity.
6 to 4 months:	Prepare prize list and entry form.
	Set closing date.
	Solicit advertising for prize list and program.

Order ribbons and trophies.

Advance ticket sales.

Print prize list, entry forms.

Get out flyers, advertise in publications.

4 to 2 months: Mail prize list and entry forms.
Distribute to places of exposure.

Send prize lists and entry forms to sanctioning associations, judges, stewards, and all show personnel.

Line up ring crews and first aid people.

Line up food concessions, and other concessionaires.

Get all other necessary printing done.

Order exhibitors' numbers.

Check grounds for any unexpected preparation that may be needed.

Line up all needed special equipment, such as jumps, etc.

Line up any special entertainment.

2 months to closing date: Committee meetings to coordinate operations and to check to see that everything is under control.

Closing date to show time: Ring and arena preparation.

See that all equipment is on hand, including public address system.

Prepare work sheets, judges' cards, exhibitors' envelopes.

Final lists of class entries, exhibi-

tors, schedule and index for pro-
gram to program chairman.
Dry run on setting up and remov-
ing jumps and trail equipment.
Check lights, if used.
Be sure stabling and feed is ready.
Place directional markers in stra-
tegic locations.
Set up show secretary's office and
announcer's booth.
Check all ribbons and trophies to
see that the order is correct.
Check exercise area.
Check parking area and attend-
ants.
Check ticket sales booths.
Make sure that everyone needing
it has enough money on hand to
make change.

This is a timing schedule from the idea of the show to
its beginning. By using it and the organizational chart
one should be reminded of everything that has to be done.

Smaller shows or affairs can move this schedule up so
that most everything can be done in a six- to four-month
period. Asking for approvals, obtaining good judges, getting dates that won't conflict, being sure of the location—
all these should be done as early as possible. Even a mall
playday takes a certain amount of time to prepare.

Remember, it is never too early to start getting ready.
There are many, many matters that must be considered
and acted upon. Smooth timing will keep the preparations on an even keel and will prevent things from piling
up at the last minute. Everyone on the committee should

know exactly what he is to do and when, and at the same time he should have a general idea of what the other committee members will be doing.

A knowledgeable chairman, aided by an informed and active committee, can put on an excellent equine affair. It merely takes thoroughness plus an untiring effort.

APPENDIX P
ORGANIZATIONAL DIAGRAM

By permission of the American Horse Shows Association, the organizational diagram for putting on a horse show is reproduced. This is from its pamphlet, *How to Operate a Horse Show*, a 14-page brochure that touches on the highlights of what concerns management.

No matter how large or how small, no matter what kind of an equine event is being considered, this chart will be of great help in reminding a show manager or committee member of things that must be taken care of. Someone in charge of the smallest playdays will find reminders in this chart of everything he has to do. And the manager of a large ten-day affair will probably break a few of these categories into further subheads. There is something here for everyone.

A.H.S.A. ORGANIZATIONAL DIAGRAM

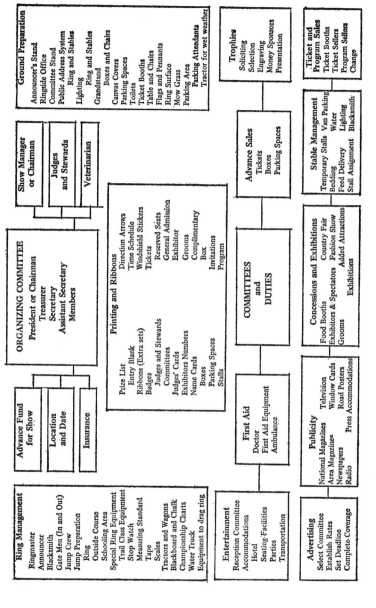

Ground Preparation
Announcer's Stand
Ringside Office
Committee Stand
Public Address System
Ring and Stables
Lighting
   Ring and Stables
Grandstand
   Boxes and Chairs
Canvas Covers
Parking Spaces
Toilets
Ticket Booths
Table and Chairs
Flags and Pennants
Ring Surface
Mow Grass
Parking Area
   Parking Attendants
   Tractor for wet weather

Show Manager or Chairman

Judges and Stewards

Veterinarian

ORGANIZING COMMITTEE
President or Chairman
Treasurer
Secretary
Assistant Secretary
Members

Advance Fund for Show

Location and Date

Insurance

Ring Management
Ringmaster
Announcer
Blacksmith
Gate Men (In and Out)
Jump Crew
Jump Preparation
Ring
Outside Course
Schooling Area
Special Ring Equipment
Trail Class Equipment
Stop Watch
Measuring Standard
Tape
Scales
Tractors and Wagons
Blackboard and Chalk
Championship Charts
Water Truck
Equipment to drag ring

Printing and Ribbons
Prize List   Direction Arrows
Entry Blank   Time Schedule
Ribbons (Extra sets)   Windshield Stickers
Badges   Tickets
Judges and Stewards   Reserved Seats
Committees   General Admission
Judges' Cards   Exhibitor
Exhibitors Numbers   Grooms
Name Cards   Complimentary
Boxes   Box
Parking Spaces   Invitations
Stalls   Program

COMMITTEES and DUTIES

Trophies
Soliciting
Selection
Engraving
Money Sponsors
Presentation

Advance Sales
Tickets
Boxes
Parking Spaces

Ticket and Program Sales
Ticket Booths
Ticket Sellers
Program Sellers
Change

Stable Management
Temporary Stalls Van Parking
Bedding Water
Feed Delivery Lighting
Stall Assignment Blacksmith

Concessions and Exhibitions
Food Booths Country Fair
Exhibitors & Spectators Fashion Show
Grooms Added Attractions
  Exhibitions

First Aid
Doctor
First Aid Equipment
Ambulance

Publicity
National Magazines Television
Area Magazines Window Cards
Newspapers Road Posters
Radio Press Accommodations

Entertainment
Reception Committee
Accommodations
Hotel
Seating-Facilities
Parties
Transportation

Advertising
Select Committee
Establish Rates
Set Deadline
Complete Coverage

Index

197